Contents

Introduction iv

The Running Example .... *v*

Alphabetization .... *vii*

Technical Issues .... *vii*

Acknowledgments ....*xi*

The Dictionary 1

A 3

B 15

C 23

D 37

E 55

F 67

G 77

H 81

I 83

J 99

K 101

L 103

M 107

N 113

O 119

P 127

Q 141

R 143

S 161

T 181

U 201

V 209

W 213

X 215

Copyright 216

The Relational Database Dictionary, Extended Edition

by C. J. Date

Thy gift, thy tables, are within my brain
Full charactered with lasting memory,
Which shall above that idle rank remain
Beyond all date, even to eternity

—William Shakespeare: *Sonnet 122*

——— ♦ ♦ ♦ ♦ ♦ ———

"When I *use a word," Humpty Dumpty said, in rather a scornful tone,*
"it means just what I choose it to mean—neither more nor less."

—Lewis Carroll: *Through the Looking-Glass and What Alice Found There*

——— ♦ ♦ ♦ ♦ ♦ ———

Lexicographer *A writer of dictionaries, a harmless drudge*

—Dr Johnson: *A Dictionary of the English Language*

——— ♦ ♦ ♦ ♦ ♦ ———

To all keepers of the true relational flame

Introduction

This dictionary contains just over 900 entries dealing with issues, terms, and concepts involved in, or arising from use of, the relational model of data. Many of the entries include not only a definition as such but also an illustrative example (sometimes more than one). With regard to those definitions, I've done my best to make them as clear, precise, and accurate as possible; they're based on my own best understanding of the material, an understanding I've gradually been honing over nearly 40 years of involvement in this field.

I'd like to stress the point that the dictionary is, as advertised, relational. To that end, I've deliberately omitted many terms and concepts that are only tangentially connected to relational matters (e.g., almost all details of the supporting type theory, including type inheritance details in particular). For the most part, I've also omitted various topics that are part of database technology in general and aren't peculiar to relational databases (e.g., security issues, the log, recovery and concurrency control, and so forth). What's more, I've also omitted certain SQL terms and concepts that—the fact that SQL is supposed to be a relational language notwithstanding—aren't really relational at all (outer join, UNION ALL, and updating through a cursor are examples). That said, I should add that I have deliberately included a few nonrelational terms in order to make it clear that, contrary to popular opinion, the concepts in question are indeed not relational (index is a case in point here).

I must explain too that this is a dictionary with an attitude. It's my very firm belief that the relational model is the right and proper foundation for database technology and will remain so for as far out as anyone can see, and many of the definitions in what follows reflect this belief. As I said in my book Database in Depth: Relational Theory for Practitioners *(O'Reilly Media Inc., 2005):*

> *[It's] my opinion that the relational model is rock solid, and "right," and will endure. A hundred years from now, I fully expect database systems still to be based on Codd's relational model. Why? Because the foundations of that model—namely, set theory and predicate logic—are themselves rock solid in turn. Elements of predicate logic in particular go back well over 2000 years, at least as far as Aristotle (384–322 BCE).*

In addition, I haven't hesitated to mark some term or concept as deprecated if I believe there are good reasons to avoid it, even if the term or concept in question is in widespread use at the time of writing. Materialized view *is a case in point here.*

The Running Example

Examples to illustrate the definitions are based for the most part on the familiar—not to say hackneyed—suppliers-and-parts database. I apologize for dragging out this old warhorse yet one more time, but I believe that using the same example in a variety of different publications can be a help, not a hindrance, in learning. Here are the relvar definitions (and if you don't know what a relvar is, then please check the dictionary entry for that term!):

```
VAR S BASE RELATION
   { S# S#, SNAME NAME, STATUS INTEGER, CITY CHAR }
     KEY { S# } ;

VAR P BASE RELATION
   { P# P#, PNAME NAME, COLOR COLOR,
                        WEIGHT WEIGHT, CITY CHAR }
     KEY { P# } ;

VAR SP BASE RELATION
   { S# S#, P# P#, QTY QTY }
     KEY { S#, P# } ;
```

The semantics are as follows:

- *Relvar S represents suppliers under contract. Each supplier has one supplier number (S#), unique to that supplier; one name (SNAME), not necessarily unique; one status value (STATUS); and one location (CITY). Attributes S#, SNAME, STATUS, and CITY are of types S#, NAME, INTEGER, and CHAR, respectively.*

- *Relvar P represents kinds of parts. Each kind of part has one part number (P#), which is unique; one name (PNAME); one color (COLOR); one weight (WEIGHT); and one location where parts of that kind are stored (CITY).*

Attributes P#, PNAME, COLOR, WEIGHT, and CITY are of types P#, NAME, COLOR, WEIGHT, and CHAR, respectively.

- *Relvar SP represents shipments (it shows which parts are shipped, or supplied, by which suppliers). Each shipment has one supplier number (S#), one part number (P#), and one quantity (QTY); there is at most one shipment at any given time for a given supplier and given part. Attributes S#, P#, and QTY are of types S#, P#, and QTY, respectively.*

Figure 1 shows a set of sample values. Examples in the body of the dictionary assume these specific values, where it makes any difference.

Figure 1. The Suppliers-and-Parts Database—Sample Values

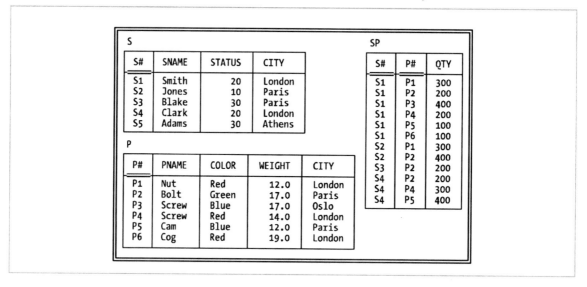

Alphabetization

For alphabetization purposes, I've followed these rules:

1. *Punctuation symbols (parentheses, hyphens, underscores, etc.) are treated as blanks.*

2. *Uppercase precedes lowercase.*

3. *Numerals precede letters.*

4. *Blanks precede everything else.*

Technical Issues

1. *Keywords, variable names, and the like are set in all uppercase throughout.*

2. *Coding examples are expressed (mostly) in a language called **Tutorial D**. I believe those examples are reasonably self-explanatory, but in any case the **Tutorial D** language is largely defined in the dictionary itself, in the entries for the various relational operators (union, join, restriction, etc.). A comprehensive description of the language can be found if needed in the book* Databases, Types, and the Relational Model: The Third Manifesto *(3rd edition), by C. J. Date and Hugh Darwen (Addison-Wesley, 2006).* Note: *As the subtitle indicates, that book also introduces and explains* The Third Manifesto, *a precise though somewhat formal definition of the relational model and a supporting type theory (including a comprehensive model of type inheritance). In particular, it uses the name **D** as a generic name for any language that conforms to the principles laid down by* The Third Manifesto. *Any number of distinct languages could qualify as a valid **D**; sadly, however, SQL isn't one of them, which is why examples in this dictionary are expressed in **Tutorial D** and not SQL. (**Tutorial D** is, of course, a valid **D**.)*

3. *Following on from the previous point, I should make it clear that all relational definitions in this dictionary are intended to conform fully to the relational model as defined by* The Third Manifesto. *As a consequence, you might find certain aspects of those definitions a trifle surprising—for example, the assertion in the entry for deferred checking that such checking is logically flawed. As I've said, this is a dictionary with an attitude.*

4. *It has become standard practice in the industry to use terms such as projection, join, and so on in two somewhat different senses: they're used to refer both to the operators identified by those names and also to the results obtained when those operators are invoked. I've followed this practice myself in this dictionary on occasion, and hope it won't lead to confusion.*

5. *It has also become standard practice in the industry to interpret the terms projection, join, and so on in another sense as well. By definition, these operators apply to relation values specifically. In particular, of course, they apply to the values that happen to be the current values of relvars. It thus clearly makes sense to talk about, e.g., the join of relvars R1 and R2, meaning the relation that results from taking the join of the current values r1 and r2, respectively, of those two relvars. In some contexts, however (normalization, for example), it turns out to be convenient to use expressions like "the join of relvars R1 and R2" in a slightly different sense. To be specific, we might say, loosely but very conveniently, that some relvar (RJ, say) is the join of relvars R1 and R2—meaning, more precisely, that the value of RJ at all times is the join of the values of R1 and R2 at the time in question. In a sense, therefore, we can talk in terms of joins of relvars per se, rather than just in terms of joins of current values of relvars. Analogous remarks apply to all of the relational operations.*

6. *Mention of projection raises yet another point. The dictionary defines projection thus:*

   Let r be a relation and let {X} be a subset of the heading of r. Then the projection of r on {X}, r{X}, is a relation with heading {X} and body consisting of all tuples x such that there exists some tuple t in r with X value x.

*But this definition isn't quite as precise as it might be. To be specific, if {X} is a subset of the heading of r, then by definition it's a set of <attribute name, type name> pairs. But in the **Tutorial D** expression r{X}, the symbol {X} is supposed to denote, not a set of <attribute name, type name> pairs, but rather just a set of attribute names. (The **Tutorial D** syntax works because attribute names are unique within the pertinent heading, and the corresponding type names are thus specified implicitly.) So there's a kind of punning going on here: The very same symbol {X} must be understood in a slightly different sense in different contexts. I hope this tiny sleight of hand on my part won't cause you any confusion, since I've made extensive use of it throughout the dictionary.* Note: *In the same kind of way, the term attribute must sometimes be understood to mean an attribute name instead of an attribute as such, and the term heading must sometimes be understood to mean a set of attribute names instead of a set of <attribute name, type name> pairs. See, for example, the entry for candidate key, which illustrates both of these usages.*

7. *Certain definitions—of certain operators, for example—require certain values to be of certain specific types. For simplicity, I haven't bothered to spell this fact out in detail in every case but have simply assumed the requirement is satisfied wherever necessary.*

8. *Several definitions and examples make use of a simplified notation for tuples. For example, consider the SP tuple shown in Figure 1 for supplier S1 and part P1. A formal **Tutorial D** representation of that tuple might look like this:*

```
TUPLE { S# S#('S1'), P# P#('P1'), QTY QTY(300) }
```

In the simplified notation under discussion, however, the same tuple would be represented thus:

```
<S1,P1,300>
```

9. *The notion of* set *is ubiquitous in the database world. On paper, a set is usually represented by a comma-separated list (or "commalist") of symbols denoting the elements, the whole enclosed in braces, as here: {a,b,c}. Throughout this dictionary, therefore, I use braces to enclose commalists of items when the items in question are meant to denote the elements of some*

set, *implying among other things that (a) the order in which the items appear within that commalist is immaterial and (b) if an item appears more than once, it's treated as if it appeared just once.*

10. *The notion of* logic *is also ubiquitous in the database world. The relational model in particular is firmly based on logic. More precisely, it's based on conventional two-valued predicate logic, 2VL (q.v.), and all references to logic in this dictionary should be taken as referring to that logic specifically, except where the context demands otherwise.* Note: *As this point suggests, many of the dictionary entries have to do with concepts from logic. Unfortunately, logic texts (and logicians) vary widely, not just in the terminology they use but also, in some cases, in the substance of their definitions. The definitions I give are the ones I find most appropriate myself, but be warned that they're sometimes at odds with others you can find in the literature.*

11. A remark on the extended edition: *It's a fact of life that dictionaries always expand from one edition to the next. The first edition of this dictionary had just over 600 entries; this one has over 900—an almost 50 percent increase. New entries include atomic relvar, attribute reference, cardinality constraint, class, computational completeness, connection trap, default, field, Great Divide, overriding, referential cycle, safe expression, stored procedure, and many others. I've also taken the opportunity to improve (and in a few cases correct) several of the existing entries; examples here include derived relation, fifth normal form, foreign key, JD implied by superkeys, NAND, NOR, ordering, and pointer. No entries have been removed!*

12. *One thing I was slightly surprised to discover in working on this extended edition was the extent to which database concepts rely, ultimately, on certain mathematical terms and constructs. As a result, I decided to include a few somewhat mathematical entries; examples here include Boolean algebra, group, inverse, nonnegative, partial ordering, and mathematical (as opposed to relational model) definitions for relation and tuple. The relevance of such entries might not be immediately apparent, but I felt it was useful to collect them together into one place in order to serve as a convenient reference for anyone who wishes to delve a little more deeply into the precise meaning and origins of a term like* relational algebra *(or the term* relation *itself, come to that).*

Acknowledgments

This dictionary was Jonathan Gennick's brainchild. Indeed, Jonathan originally intended to write it himself, and I'm very grateful to him for stepping out of the limelight, as it were, and letting me steal his idea and run with it as I've done. Jonathan and I have very different writing styles, and what follows is no doubt a long way from what he originally had in mind; but I hope it at least does justice to his overall idea. I'd also like to thank O'Reilly Media Inc. (publishers of the first edition) for allowing me to place this extended edition with a different publisher, and my friend and colleague Hugh Darwen for numerous helpful comments on earlier drafts and much other technical assistance. Of course, it goes without saying that any remaining errors and infelicities are my own responsibility. Finally, I'd like to thank the team at Apress for their professionalism and their efforts in getting this book out so expeditiously. It has been a pleasure to work with them.

The Dictionary

0-adic Niladic.

0-ary Nullary.

0-tuple The empty tuple.

1NF First normal form.

2NF Second normal form.

2VL Two-valued logic.

3NF Third normal form.

3VL Three-valued logic.

4NF Fourth normal form.

5NF Fifth normal form.

6NF Sixth normal form.

A

A A relationally complete, "reduced instruction set" form of relational algebra with just two primitive operator—REMOVE (essentially projection on all attributes but one) and an algebraic analog of either NOR or NAND, q.v. The name is a doubly recursive acronym: It stands for *ALGEBRA,* which in turn stands for *A Logical Genesis Explains Basic Relational Algebra.* As this expanded name suggests, it is designed in such a way as to emphasize its close relationship to, and solid foundation in, the discipline of predicate logic, q.v. Further details can be found in the book *Databases, Types, and the Relational Model: The Third Manifesto* (3rd edition), by C. J. Date and Hugh Darwen (Addison-Wesley, 2006). *Note*: That book uses solid arrowheads, ◄ and ►, to delimit **A** operator names, as in ◄NOR►, in order to distinguish those operators from operators with the same name in predicate logic or **Tutorial D** or both, but those arrowheads are deliberately omitted here. More to the point, that book doesn't actually define either NOR or NAND as a primitive **A** operator; rather, it defines **A** as including explicit NOT, OR, and AND operators. But it then goes on to show that (a) either OR or AND could be removed without loss, and (b) NOT and whichever of OR and AND is retained could be collapsed into a single operator—NOT and OR into NOR, or NOT and AND into NAND. So no serious harm is done by thinking of either NOR or NAND (like REMOVE, q.v.) as a primitive operator of **A**.

Abelian group *See* group (mathematics).

absolute complement *See* complement (set theory).

absorption Let operators *OpC* and *OpD* both be dyadic, and assume for definiteness that they're expressed in infix style. Then *OpC* absorbs *OpD* if and only if, for all *x* and *y*, *x OpC* (*x OpD y*) = *x*.

Examples: In logic, OR and AND each absorb the other, because *x* OR (*x* AND *y*) and *x* AND (*x* OR *y*) both reduce to just *x*. Similarly, in set theory and relational algebra, union and intersection each absorb the other.

abstract data type Type. *Note*: The term is sometimes used to refer to some specific kind of type (especially one that isn't built in), but a strong case can be made that all types are or should be "abstract," at least in the sense that their physical representation is hidden from the user.

access path An implementation construct. Typical examples include hashes, indexes, and pointer chains. There are no access paths in the relational model—all access to relations is via associative addressing, q.v.

actual operand *See* argument.

ad hoc polymorphism *See* overloading.

aggregate operator A read-only operator that derives a single value, typically but not necessarily a scalar value, from the "aggregate" (i.e., the set or bag) of values appearing as values of some attribute of some relation—or, in the case of COUNT, which is slightly special, from the "aggregate" that's the entire relation as such. *Contrast* summary. *Note*: If (a) some aggregate operator invocation is such that the relation over which the aggregation is to be done is empty, and (b) that invocation is essentially just shorthand for repeated invocation of some dyadic scalar operator, and (c) an identity value, q.v., exists for that scalar operator, then the result of that invocation is that identity value. For example, suppose the operator SUM is invoked on an aggregate consisting of a set of values of type INTEGER. Since SUM is essentially just shorthand for repeated invocation of the scalar operator "+", and an identity value—namely, zero—exists for "+" on integers, the result if the aggregate is empty is zero.

Example: Let ST be a variable of type INTEGER. Then the following statement assigns to ST the sum of the status values for suppliers in London:

```
ST := SUM ( S WHERE CITY = 'London', STATUS ) ;
```

STATUS here is an attribute reference (q.v.). And if relvar S is currently empty, then after this assignment variable ST will have the value zero.

ALGEBRA *See* A.

algebra 1. Generically, a formal system consisting of a set of elements and a set of read-only operators that together satisfy certain laws and properties (certainly closure, probably commutativity and associativity, and so on); also known as an algebraic structure or an abstract algebra. The word *algebra* itself derives from Arabic *al-jebr,* meaning a resetting (of something broken) or a combination. *See also* Boolean algebra; field (mathematics); group (mathematics); Laws of Algebra, The; relational algebra; ring (mathematics). 2. Relational algebra specifically (if the context demands).

algebra of sets *See* Boolean algebra (second definition).

alias Deprecated term used in some SQL products to mean either a tuple calculus range variable or the name of such a variable. The term *table alias* (also deprecated) is also sometimes used with the same meaning.

ALL BUT *See* projection.

ALPHA A proposal, due to Codd, for a concrete relational language based on tuple calculus; also known as Data Sublanguage ALPHA. ALPHA was never implemented, but its ideas were influential on the design of several languages that were, including QBE, QUEL, and (to a much lesser extent) SQL.

alternate key Loosely, a candidate key that isn't the primary key. More precisely, let relvar R have keys $K1, K2, \ldots, Kn$, and let some Ki ($i = 1, 2, \ldots, n$) be chosen as the primary key for R; then each Kj ($j = 1, 2, \ldots, n, j \neq i$) is an alternate key for R. The term isn't much used.

AND *See* conjunction. *Note*: AND as conventionally understood is a logical operator; however, the algebra **A**, q.v., includes an operator it calls AND that—by definition—is an algebraic operator (in fact, it's just natural join).

antecedent *See* implication.

antisymmetry *See* partial ordering. Note that there's a logical difference between antisymmetry and asymmetry; the former is as defined under partial ordering, while the latter just means lack of symmetry.

appearance *(Of a value)* An occurrence or "instance" of a value (in some context). Observe that there's a logical difference between a value as such and an appearance of that value—for example, an appearance as the current value of some variable or as an attribute value within the current value of some tuplevar or some relvar. Each such appearance consists internally of some physical representation of the value in question (and distinct appearances of the same value might have distinct physical representations). Thus, there's also a logical difference between an appearance of a value, on the one hand, and the physical representation of that appearance, on the other; there might even be a logical difference between the physical representations used for distinct appearances of the same value. All of that being said, however, it's usual to abbreviate *physical representation of an appearance of a value* to just *appearance of a value,* or (more often) just *value,* so long as there's no risk of ambiguity. Note that *appearance of a value* is a model concept, whereas *physical representation of an appearance* is an implementation concept—users certainly might need to know whether (for example) two variables contain appearances of the same value, but they don't need to know whether those appearances use the same physical representation.

Example: Let N1 and N2 be variables of type INTEGER. After the following assignments, then, N1 and N2 both contain an appearance of the integer value 3. The corresponding physical representations might or might not be the same (for example, N1 might use a base two representation and N2 a base ten representation), but it's of no concern to the user either way.

```
N1  :=  3  ;
N2  :=  3  ;
```

application relvar *See* relvar.

argument An actual operand that replaces some parameter of some operator when that operator is invoked. Note that there's a logical difference between an argument per se and the expression that denotes it (i.e., the argument expression). The argument per se is either a value or a variable. If the pertinent parameter is subject to update, then the argument is—in fact, must be—a variable, denoted by some variable reference; otherwise it's a value and can be denoted by an arbitrarily complex expression (possibly just a variable reference). *Contrast* parameter.

Examples: Let operator DOUBLE be defined as follows:

```
OPERATOR DOUBLE ( X INTEGER ) RETURNS INTEGER ;
   RETURN ( 2 * X ) ;
END OPERATOR ;
```

X here is a parameter, of declared type INTEGER. Let N be a variable of type INTEGER. Then, e.g., DOUBLE(N+1) is an invocation of DOUBLE, and the value of the expression N+1 at the time of that invocation is an argument—in fact, the sole argument—to that invocation. That invocation is itself an expression in turn, and it can appear wherever an integer literal can appear (because operator DOUBLE is defined to return a value of type INTEGER).

Suppose now that DOUBLE is defined to be an update operator instead of a read-only one:

```
OPERATOR DOUBLE ( X INTEGER ) UPDATES { X } ;
    X := 2 * X ;
END OPERATOR ;
```

Now the parameter X is subject to update, and any argument corresponding to X must be a variable. Thus, e.g., DOUBLE(N) is a valid invocation of DOUBLE, and the variable N—not the value of that variable, observe—is the argument to that invocation. (Note that, e.g., DOUBLE(N+1) would be a syntax error, because N+1 isn't a variable reference.) However, that invocation DOUBLE(N) isn't an expression, and it can't appear "wherever an integer literal can appear"; instead, it can appear only in an explicit CALL statement (or equivalent), as here:

```
CALL DOUBLE ( N ) ;
```

argument expression An expression denoting an argument, q.v.

arity Degree, q.v. The term isn't much used.

Armstrong's inference rules (*For FDs*) Let *A, B,* and *C* be subsets of the heading of some relvar. Let *AC* denote the set theory union of *A* and *B,* and similarly for *BC.* Then Armstrong's rules (also known as Armstrong's axioms) state that (a) if *A* is a superset of *B,* then $A \rightarrow B$ (the reflexivity rule); (b) if $A \rightarrow B$, then $AC \rightarrow BC$ (the augmentation rule); and (c) if $A \rightarrow B$ and $B \rightarrow C$, then $A \rightarrow C$ (the transitivity rule). These rules are both sound and complete (*see* completeness; soundness).

Examples: Let *s* be a set of FDs, and let *s* contain the FD $A \rightarrow BC$. Then the FD $A \rightarrow B$ is implied by *s* and can easily be derived using Armstrong's rules as follows: (a) $A \rightarrow BC$ (given); (b) $BC \rightarrow B$ (reflexivity); hence (c) $A \rightarrow B$ (transitivity).

By way of a second example, if the set *s* contains the FDs $A \rightarrow B$ and $C \rightarrow D$, then the FD $AX \rightarrow BD$ (where *X* is the set theory difference between *C* and *B,* in that order) is implied by *s*. *Note*: This example, which is due to Darwen, can be regarded as another inference rule. It has the interesting property that the augmentation and transitivity rules, as well as several other rules not discussed here, are all special cases.

arrow *See* functional dependency.

assignment An operator that assigns a value (the source, denoted by an expression) to a variable (the target, denoted by a variable reference); also, the operation performed when that operator is invoked. The source and target must be of the same type. *Note*: Every update operator invocation is semantically equivalent to some assignment operation (possibly a multiple assignment, q.v.).

Assignment Principle, The After assignment of value v to variable V, the comparison $v = V$ is required to evaluate to TRUE.

associative addressing Addressing by value instead of position. All addressing is associative in the relational model, implying among other things that pointers, q.v., are explicitly rejected.

associativity Let Op be a dyadic operator, and assume for definiteness that Op is expressed in infix style. Then Op is associative if and only if, for all $x, y,$ and $z, x\ Op\ (y\ Op\ z) = (x\ Op\ y)\ Op\ z$.

Examples: In ordinary arithmetic, addition ("+") is associative, because

$$x + (y + z) = (x + y) + z$$

for all numbers $x, y,$ and z. Likewise, "||" (string concatenation) is associative, because

$$x \ || \ (y \ || \ z) = (x \ || \ y) \ || \ z$$

for all strings $x, y,$ and z. In the same kind of way, UNION and JOIN are associative in relational algebra (by contrast, MINUS is not). Likewise, OR and AND are associative in logic (by contrast, IMPLIES is not). *Note*: All of the associative operators just mentioned except "||" are also commutative, q.v. Another example of an operator that's associative but not commutative is the unnamed dyadic connective in two-valued logic that simply returns the value of its first argument. *See also* left associativity; right associativity.

atomic predicate A simple predicate, q.v.

atomic proposition A simple proposition, q.v.

atomic relvar Deprecated term for a relvar that can't be decomposed into independent projections (*see* FD preservation). The term is deprecated because it's likely to be confused with the term *irreducible relvar* (*see* irreducibility, second definition). While it's true that irreducible relvars are always atomic, the converse is false—a relvar can be atomic without being irreducible, and in fact without even being in BCNF. The concept is seldom needed, anyway; thus, it's probably best just to spell out the meaning when necessary.

Example: Suppose relvar SP satisfies the additional FD {QTY} → {P#}, meaning the part number for a given shipment is a function of the shipment quantity; e.g., part P1 (alone) is always supplied in a quantity of 100, part P2 (alone) in a quantity of 200, and so on (this example is very contrived, of course, but it suffices for the purpose at hand). This revised version of SP isn't in BCNF (because {QTY} isn't a superkey), and it can be nonloss decomposed into its projections on {S#,QTY} and {QTY,P#}. However, those projections, though they're in BCNF, aren't independent, because the FD {S#,P#} → {QTY} isn't preserved in the decomposition; this revised version of SP is thus not atomic. *Note*: It follows from this example that the objectives of (a) decomposing into BCNF projections and (b) decomposing into atomic projections, though both generally desirable, can sometimes be in conflict.

atomic statement (*Programming languages*) Syntactically, a statement that contains no other statements nested inside itself (*contrast* compound statement); semantically, a statement that is guaranteed either to execute in its entirety or to have no effect, except possibly for returning a status code or equivalent. All syntactically atomic statements are semantically atomic in the relational model. (The converse is false, incidentally; to be specific, multiple assignment, q.v., is semantically but not syntactically atomic.)

atomic type Deprecated term for a scalar type. *See* scalar.

atomic value Old fashioned and somewhat deprecated term for a scalar value. *See* scalar.

attribute Loosely, a column; more precisely, an <attribute name, type name> pair, though it's common to refer to a given attribute informally by its attribute name alone. (This simplified form is acceptable because the relational model requires attribute names to be unique within the pertinent heading, and those names thus effectively imply the corresponding type names.)

Examples: In the suppliers-and-parts database, (a) the pair <SNAME,NAME> is an attribute of relvar S; (b) the pair <S#,S#> is an attribute—a "common attribute," q.v.—of both relvar S and relvar SP. We might also say, more simply but less formally, just that (a) SNAME is an attribute of relvar S and (b) S# is an attribute—a "common attribute"—of both relvar S and relvar SP. These two attributes are of types NAME and S#, respectively.

attribute assignment *See* attribute reference.

attribute constraint A specification (conceptually part of a relvar constraint, q.v.) to the effect that a given attribute of a given relvar is of a given declared type.

Example: Attribute SNAME of relvar S is declared to be of type NAME—that is, it's constrained to contain values of type NAME. Any operation that attempts to introduce an SNAME value into that relvar that's not of that type will immediately fail.

attribute extractor An operator for extracting the value of a specified attribute from a specified tuple.

Example: Let *t* denote the supplier tuple in Figure 1 for supplier S1. Then the following expression extracts the status value 20 (an integer) from that tuple:

```
STATUS FROM t
```

STATUS here is an attribute reference, q.v.

attribute FROM Tutorial D syntax for an attribute extractor, q.v.

attribute reference Syntactically, an attribute name (possibly dot qualified). An attribute reference denotes either an attribute as such or the value of the attribute in question (usually though not always within some specific tuple in each case), as the context demands. Note in particular that such a reference certainly denotes an attribute as such if it appears on the left side of an "attribute assignment" within some UPDATE operator invocation.

Examples: Consider the following UPDATE statement:

```
UPDATE P WHERE CITY = 'London' :
        { WEIGHT := 2 * WEIGHT , CITY := 'Oslo' } ;
```

This statement contains two attribute assignments and four attribute references, CITY (twice) and WEIGHT (also twice). Imagine the overall UPDATE being executed by processing the tuples of relvar P one by one in some sequence, and let *t* be the tuple currently being processed. Within the overall statement, then, (a) the first appearance of CITY and the second appearance of WEIGHT denote the CITY value and the WEIGHT value, respectively, within *t*; (b) the first appearance of WEIGHT and the second appearance of CITY denote the WEIGHT attribute as such and the CITY attribute as such, respectively, within *t*. *See* UPDATE for further explanation.

attribute renaming *See* renaming.

attribute type *See* attribute.

attribute value *See* tuple value.

augmentation *See* Armstrong's inference rules.

axiom Something assumed to be true, available for use in deriving further truths (i.e., theorems, q.v.). In a database, the tuples in the base relations can be regarded as axioms, because they represent propositions that are assumed to be true. An axiom is a special case of a theorem. *See* proof.

Example: The tuple <S1,Smith,20,London> in the relation that's the current value of base relvar S represents the presumably true proposition "Supplier S1 is under contract, is named Smith, has status 20, and is located in London."

axiom of extension An axiom of set theory, to the effect that two sets are equal if and only if they have the same elements (in which case they are in fact the same set).

B

bag Very loosely, a "set" that permits duplicates; more precisely, a collection of objects, called elements, in which the same element can appear any number of times. An example is the collection (y,y,x,z,y,z), which can equivalently be written as (x,y,y,y,z,z), since bags, like sets, have no ordering to their elements. The number of times a given element appears in a given bag is the multiplicity (of that element with respect to that bag).

The set theory operations of inclusion, union, intersection, difference, and product (but not complement) can all be generalized to apply to bags. First, inclusion: Let $b1$ and $b2$ be bags, and let element x appear exactly $n1$ times in $b1$ and exactly $n2$ times in $b2$ ($n1 \geq 0$, $n2 \geq 0$). Then bag $b1$ includes bag $b2$ ($b1 \supseteq b2$) if and only if $n1 \geq n2$ for all such elements x; further, $b2$ is included in $b1$ ($b2 \subseteq b1$) if and only if $b1$ includes $b2$, and $b1$ is equal to $b2$ ($b1 = b2$) if and only if each includes the other. All of the terms associated with set inclusion (superset, subset, and so on) have analogs in connection with bag inclusion (superbag, subbag, and so on).

Now let Op be union, intersection, or difference, and let b be the bag obtained by applying Op to bags $b1$ and $b2$ (in that order, in the case of difference), where as before element x appears exactly $n1$ times in $b1$ and exactly $n2$ times in $b2$ ($n1 \geq 0$, $n2 \geq 0$). Then element x appears exactly n times in b, where n is:

- MAX($n1,n2$) if Op is union
- MIN($n1,n2$) if Op is intersection
- MAX($n1-n2,0$) if Op is difference

In no case does b contain any other elements.

Now let elements $x1$ and $x2$ appear exactly $n1$ times in $b1$ and exactly $n2$ times in $b2$, respectively ($n1 \geq 0$, $n2 \geq 0$), and let b be the product of $b1$ and *b2*, in that order. Then the pair $<x1,x2>$ appears exactly $n1*n2$ times in *b*, and *b* contains no other elements.

Finally, there are two operations, union plus and intersection star (also known by a variety of other names), that have no counterpart in set theory. Let *b* be the bag obtained by applying one of these operations to bags *b1* and *b2*, where once again element *x* appear exactly *n1* times in *b1* and exactly *n2* times in *b2* ($n1 \geq 0$, $n2 \geq 0$). Then element *x* appears exactly *n* times in *b*, where *n* is:

- $n1+n2$ if *Op* is union plus
- $n1*n2$ if *Op* is intersection star

Note: SQL supports union plus but not true bag union. It does not support intersection star.

Examples: Let *b1* and *b2* be the bags (w,w,x,x,y) and (x,y,y,y,z,z), respectively. Then the following expressions yield the indicated results:

- `b1 UNION b2` = (w,w,x,x,y,y,y,z,z)
- `b1 INTERSECT b2` = (x,y)
- `b1 MINUS b2` = (w,w,x)
- `b2 MINUS b1` = (y,y,z,z)
- `b1 TIMES b2` = $(<w,x>,<w,x>,<x,x>,<x,x>,<y,x>,$
$<w,y>,<w,y>,<x,y>,<x,y>,<y,y>,$
$<w,y>,<w,y>,<x,y>,<x,y>,<y,y>,$
$<w,y>,<w,y>,<x,y>,<x,y>,<y,y>,$
$<w,z>,<w,z>,<x,z>,<x,z>,<y,z>,$
$<w,z>,<w,z>,<x,z>,<x,z>,<y,z>)$
- `b1 UNION+ b2` = (w,w,x,x,x,y,y,y,y,z,z)
- `b1 INTERSECT* b2` = (x,x,y,y,y)

bag inclusion *See* bag.

bag membership (*Of an element*) The property of appearing in some given bag; the operation of testing for that property. Like set membership, q.v., bag membership is usually denoted by the symbol "∈"; thus, the Boolean expression $x \in b$ returns TRUE if and only if element x does in fact appear at least once in bag b.

bag operator *See* bag.

base relation The value of a given base relvar at a given time. *Contrast* derived relation.

Examples: The relations that are the values of relvars S, P, and SP at any given time.

base relvar A relvar not defined in terms of others; that is, an independent relvar. *Contrast* derived relvar. *Note*: It's a popular misconception that base relvars are physically stored, in the sense that they're represented in storage by physical files and their tuples and attributes are represented in storage by records and fields within those files (*see* direct image). But the relational model deliberately has nothing to say about physical storage; in particular, it categorically doesn't say that base relvars, as such, are physically stored—neither in the foregoing sense, nor in any other. The only requirement is that there must be some defined mapping from what's physically stored to what's perceived by the user (i.e., base relvars or derived relvars or a mixture of both) and vice versa.

Examples: Relvars S, P, and SP.

base table SQL analog of either a base relation or a base relvar, as the context demands. *See also* table.

BCNF Boyce/Codd normal form.

bi-implication Logical equivalence.

BI-IMPLIES Same as EQUIV.

bijection A mapping, or function, from set *s1* to set *s2* such that each element of *s2* is the image of exactly one element of *s1*; equivalently, a mapping that is both an injection and a surjection (in other words, a one-to-one correspondence, in the strict sense of that term, from *s1* to *s2*). Also known as a bijective or "one-to-one onto" mapping. Note that if a given mapping is bijective, then it has an inverse mapping that's bijective as well.

Examples: The mapping from integers *x* to their successors *x*+1 is a bijection from the set of all integers to itself. So is the inverse mapping from integers *x* to their predecessors *x*-1.

binary Of degree two.

binding (*Logic*) Converting a free variable to a bound variable by means of quantification, q.v.

body A set of tuples all of the same type; especially, the set of tuples appearing in a given relation, or in a given relvar at a given time. Every subset of a body is itself a body.

Examples: The set of tuples appearing in relvar S at any given time; any subset of that set.

BOOLEAN A scalar data type—the only one required by the relational model—containing just two values (two truth values, to be specific, denoted by the literals TRUE and FALSE, respectively).

Boolean algebra 1. (*Simple case*) The truth values TRUE and FALSE, together with the logical operators NOT, OR, and AND, q.v. 2. (*General case*) Let *s* be a set; let "≤" be a partial ordering, q.v., on *s*; and let a monadic operator "¬" (complement) and distinct dyadic operators "+"(addition) and "∗" (multiplication) be defined on *s,* such that (a) "¬" satisfies the closure and involution laws; (b) "+" and "∗" satisfy the closure, commutative, associative, distributive, idempotence, and absorption laws (meaning, in the case of the distributive law in particular, that each "+" and "∗" distributes over the other); and (c) "¬", "+", and "∗" together satisfy De Morgan's Laws. Let *s* also contain two elements 0 and

1 such that (a) 0 is the identity for "+"; (b) 1 is the identity for "∗"; and (c) for all elements x in s, $0 \leq x \leq 1$. Then the combination of s and the operators "≤", "¬", "+", and "∗" is a Boolean algebra. *Note*: Although they're usually referred to in this context as addition and multiplication, respectively, it must be clearly understood that "+" and "∗" aren't necessarily the operators known by those names in conventional arithmetic.

Example (*second definition*): Let s be an arbitrary set; let p be the power set of s; and let "≤", "¬", "+", and "∗" denote set inclusion, set complement, set union, and set intersection, respectively. Then the combination of the power set p and the operators "≤", "¬", "+", and "∗" as just defined is a Boolean algebra, in which the empty set and the set s itself serve as the required additive identity and multiplicative identity, respectively. (In other words, the familiar algebra of sets is in fact a Boolean algebra.)

Boolean expression A logical expression, q.v.

Boolean operator A read-only logical operator, q.v. (especially one of the connectives, q.v.).

Boolean value A value of type BOOLEAN, q.v.; in other words, a truth value.

bound variable In logic, a variable—more precisely, an occurrence of a variable reference within some predicate—that either (a) appears within the scope of a quantifier that explicitly specifies that variable or (b) is that explicit specification itself. (The term *variable* is used here in the sense of logic, not in the programming language sense.) *Contrast* free variable.

Examples: Let the symbols x and y denote integers. Then the following expressions are both predicates, and x appears as a bound variable, twice, in each of them:

```
EXISTS x ( x > 3 )

EXISTS x ( x > 3 ) AND y < 7
```

The first of these predicates is in fact a proposition, and its meaning is "There exists an integer x such that x is greater than three" (a proposition that evaluates to TRUE, of course). By contrast, the second predicate is not a proposition, because it involves a free variable (namely, y) as well as the two bound ones; thus, it has no truth value.

Turning to a database example, the following is a query ("Get suppliers who supply at least one part") on the suppliers-and-parts database, expressed in tuple calculus, q.v.:

```
S WHERE EXISTS SP ( SP.S# = S.S# )
```

The Boolean expression following the keyword WHERE here is a predicate, and the references to SP in that predicate are bound (by contrast, the reference to S is free). Note, however, that in this particular example the symbols S and SP denote not only variables in the sense of logic but also variables in the conventional programming language sense—but that's because we've indulged in a certain sleight of hand, as it were. Here's an extended version of the same example that should help clarify matters:

```
SX  RANGES OVER { S }  ;
SPX RANGES OVER { SP } ;

SX WHERE EXISTS SPX ( SPX.S# = SX.S# )
```

Here SX and SPX have been explicitly declared as variables in the sense of logic, ranging over (the current values of) relvars S and SP, respectively. Now it's the references to SPX that are bound and the reference to SX that's free (in the predicate following the keyword WHERE in both cases). In effect, what happened in the first version of the example was that we were appealing to a syntax rule that allowed a relvar name to be used to denote an implicitly defined range variable that ranges over (the current value of) the relvar with the same name. *Note*: SQL includes a rule of exactly this kind.

Boyce/Codd normal form   Relvar R is in Boyce/Codd normal form, BCNF, if and only if every nontrivial FD satisfied by R is implied by some superkey of R; equivalently, if and only if for every nontrivial FD $A \to B$ satisfied by R, A is a superkey for R. Every BCNF relvar is in 3NF. *Note*: BCNF is "the" normal form with respect to FDs. Also, although being in BCNF clearly doesn't preclude being in the next higher normal form (4NF) as well, the term *BCNF* is often used loosely to refer to a relvar that's in BCNF and not in 4NF.

Example: With the normal forms it's often more instructive to show a counterexample rather than an example per se. Suppose, therefore, that relvar SP has an additional attribute SNAME, representing the name of the applicable supplier; suppose also that supplier names are necessarily unique (i.e., no two suppliers ever have the same name at the same time). This revised version of SP has two keys, {S#,P#} and {SNAME,P#}, and every subset of the heading—{QTY} in particular—is (of course) functionally dependent on both of them. However, the relvar also satisfies the FDs {S#} $\to$ {SNAME} and {SNAME} $\to$ {S#}; these FDs are certainly not trivial, nor are they "arrows out of superkeys," and so the relvar isn't in BCNF (though it is in 3NF).

built in System defined. *Contrast* user defined.

business rule A statement, usually in natural language, that's supposed to capture some aspect of what the data in the database means or how its values are constrained. There's no consensus on any more precise definition of the term, but most writers would at least agree that relvar predicates, q.v., are an important special case.

C

calculus 1. Generically, a system of formal computation (the Latin word *calculus* means a pebble, perhaps used in counting or some other form of reckoning). 2. Relational calculus specifically (if the context demands).

candidate key Loosely, a unique identifier. More precisely, let K be a subset of the heading of relvar R; then K is a candidate key (key for short) for R if and only if (a) no possible value for R contains two distinct tuples with the same value for K (the uniqueness property), while (b) the same can't be said for any proper subset of K (the irreducibility property). Note that every relvar, base or derived, has at least one key. Note too that, by definition, keys are sets of attributes (and key values are therefore tuples); however, if the set of attributes constituting some key K contains just one attribute A, then it's common (though strictly incorrect) to speak informally of that attribute A per se as being that key. *Contrast* subkey; superkey. *See also* key constraint.

Examples: In the suppliers-and-parts database, {S#}, {P#}, and {S#,P#} are the sole keys for relvars S, P, and SP, respectively. Note that {SNAME} isn't a key for S, because values of {SNAME} aren't necessarily unique (though the values shown in Figure 1 do happen to be unique). Note too that, for example, {S#,CITY} isn't a key for S either, because although its values are necessarily unique, it isn't irreducible—we could remove the CITY attribute, and what would be left would still satisfy the uniqueness property. (Irreducibility is desirable because, without it, the system would be enforcing the wrong integrity constraint. In the case at hand, for example, it wouldn't be enforcing the constraint that supplier numbers are "globally" unique, but merely the weaker constraint that they're unique within each city.)

canonical form Given a set $s1$, together with a notion of equivalence among the elements of that set, subset $s2$ of $s1$ is a set of canonical forms for $s1$ if and only if every element $x1$ in $s1$ is equivalent to just one element $x2$ in $s2$ (and that element $x2$ is the canonical form for the element $x1$). Various "interesting" properties that apply to $x1$ also apply to $x2$; thus, we can study just the small set $s2$, not the large set $s1$, in order to prove a variety of "interesting" theorems or results.

Example: Let $s1$ be the set of nonnegative integers $\{0,1,2,\ldots\}$ and let two such integers be equivalent if and only if they leave the same remainder on division by five. Then we can define $s2$ to be the set $\{0,1,2,3,4\}$. As for an "interesting" theorem that applies in this example, let $x1$, $y1$, and $z1$ be any three elements of $s1$, and let their canonical forms in $s2$ be $x2$, $y2$, and $z2$, respectively; then the product $y1 * z1$ is equivalent to $x1$ if and only if the product $y2 * z2$ is equivalent to $x2$.

cardinality The number of elements in a bag or (especially) set; of a relation, the number of tuples in the body of that relation. Also used (a) of a relvar, to mean the cardinality of the relation that's the value of that relvar at a given time; (b) of an attribute of a relation or relvar, to mean the cardinality of the set of distinct values of that attribute appearing in the body of that relation or relvar—at a given time, in the case of a relvar. (Of course, the cardinality of attribute A of relation r is the same as the cardinality of the projection $r\{A\}$ of that relation on that attribute; definition (b) here is thus strictly redundant.)

Examples: In Figure 1, (a) the cardinality of the relation that's the current value of relvar SP is twelve (and the cardinality of relvar SP is thus currently twelve also); (b) the cardinality of attribute S# in that relation is 4 (and the cardinality of that attribute in relvar SP is thus currently 4 also).

cardinality constraint 1. A constraint on the cardinality of a given relvar (a special case of a relvar constraint, q.v.); for example, a constraint to the effect that there can never be more than ten suppliers at any given time.

2. Let *r* be a relationship from set *s1* to set *s2,* and let *x1* and *x2* be typical elements of *s1* and *s2,* respectively. In E/R modeling and similar design schemes, then, the following are all cardinality constraints that can be specified for each of *s1* and *s2*: 1, 0..1, 0..*m*, 1..*m* (other notations are also used). For definiteness, assume the constraint in question has been specified for set *s2*; then that constraint indicates how many *x2*'s correspond to each *x1* in relationship *r*. The various specifications have the following meanings: 1 means there must be exactly one *x2*; 0..1 means there must be at most one *x2*; 0..*m* means there can be any number of *x2*'s, from zero to some undefined upper bound *m*; and 1..*m* means there can be any number of *x2*'s, from one to some undefined upper bound *m*. *Note:* The terms *optional participation* and *mandatory participation* are sometimes used to refer to the case where the lower bound is 0 and the case where it's 1, respectively; however, there's no universal agreement on what these terms mean, and they're probably best avoided.

Cartesian join Same as Cartesian product.

Cartesian product 1. (*Dyadic case*) The Cartesian product of two relations *r1* and *r2*, *r1* TIMES *r2*, where *r1* and *r2* have no attribute names in common, is a relation with heading the set theory union of the headings of *r1* and *r2* and with body the set of all tuples *t* such that *t* is the set theory union of a tuple from *r1* and a tuple from *r2*. 2. (*N-adic case*) The Cartesian product of *n* relations *r1, r2, . . . , rn* ($n \geq 0$), TIMES {*r1,r2, . . . ,rn*}, where no two of *r1, r2, . . . , rn* have any attribute names in common, is a relation with heading the set theory union of the headings of *r1, r2, . . . , rn* and with body the set of all tuples *t* such that *t* is the set theory union of a tuple from *r1,* a tuple from *r2, . . . ,* and a tuple from *rn*. *Note:* The relational Cartesian product operator differs in several respects from the mathematical or set theory operator of the same name, q.v., and is sometimes explicitly said to be an expanded, or extended, Cartesian product for that reason. In fact, it's a special case of join, q.v.

Example: Let *r1* and *r2* be the projections S{S#} and P{P#}, respectively. Then the Cartesian product *r1* TIMES *r2* contains all possible tuples of the form <s#,p#> (where *s#* is an S# value currently appearing in relvar S and *p#* is a P# value currently appearing in relvar P), and no other tuples. (Given the values in Figure 1, the result has cardinality 30.) Note that the expression (S{S#}) TIMES (P{P#}) is semantically equivalent to the expression (S{S#}) JOIN (P{P#}).

Cartesian product (*Set theory*) The Cartesian product of two sets *s1* and *s2* is the set of all ordered pairs of elements such that the first element of the pair is an element of *s1* and the second element of the pair is an element of *s2*. *Note*: This definition can obviously be extended to apply to any number of sets.

cascading Repeating some requested update on some additional target, over and above the one specified in the update request, typically but not necessarily in order to avoid some integrity violation that would otherwise occur. *See also* compensating action.

catalog Within a given database, a set of relvars that describe that database (including the catalog relvars themselves—i.e., the catalog is self-describing). Such relvars are sometimes said to contain metadata, q.v. Catalog relvars are usually updated not by explicit assignment operations but rather by more user-friendly data definition operators, q.v. (which are nevertheless essentially just shorthand for certain relational assignments).

Cautious Design Principle, The *See* Principle of Cautious Design, The.

cell Term sometimes used to refer to a row-and-column intersection in a table; not to be confused with the content of the cell in question. Note that the concept of "cells" makes sense in connection with the idea that a table is a picture of a relation (*see* table) but not in connection with the idea that a table *is* such a relation, which is why this definition is framed in terms of tables and not relations. It's true that we might think, very informally, of some relation in terms of "tuple-and-attribute intersections," but we can't sensibly regard those intersections as being somehow distinct from their content. (Take the content away from a relation and nothing remains; as Lewis Carroll might have observed, a relation without its content would be like a grin without a cat.)

child / child table Deprecated, because inappropriate, terms sometimes used in SQL contexts to mean (the SQL analog of) a referencing relvar, q.v.

class 1. (*Mathematics*) Term usually used just as a synonym for set—though it's sometimes used in a more general sense, to include collections of elements that aren't regarded as legitimate sets for some reason. For example, the (infinite) collection of all sets is regarded by some mathematicians as a class but not a set. 2. (*OO*) Term used to mean, variously, (a) a type; (b) the implementation or physical representation of some given type; (c) a type and one of its implementations in combination; (d) the set of all values of some given type currently in use; and (e) possibly other things besides.

closed WFF A WFF that denotes a proposition. *Contrast* open WFF.

Closed World Assumption, The Loosely, the assumption that everything stated or implied by the database is true and everything else is false. More precisely, The Closed World Assumption (CWA) states that (a) if a given tuple appears in a given relvar at a given time, then the proposition represented by that tuple is true at that time, and (b) if a given tuple could appear in that relvar at that time but doesn't, then the proposition represented by that tuple is false at that time. At any given time, in other words, the relvar contains all and only those tuples that correspond to true propositions—that is, invocations, or full instantiations, of the relvar predicate that evaluate to TRUE—at that time. *Note*: The relvar in question doesn't have to be a base relvar, which is why the phrase "or implied" appears in the original loose characterization. Note too that the definition is phrased in terms of a relvar specifically, but a precisely analogous definition applies to relations also (*see* extension, third definition). *Contrast* Open World Assumption, The.

Examples: The tuple <S1,P1,300> currently appears in relvar SP; we can therefore assume that it currently is the case that supplier S1 supplies part P1 in quantity 300. By contrast, the tuple <S5,P6,250> doesn't currently appear, though presumably it could; we can therefore assume that it's currently not the case that supplier S5 supplies part P6 in quantity 250.

As for an example of implied information, observe that the tuple <S3> currently appears in the projection of relvar SP on {S#}; we can therefore assume that it currently is the case that supplier S3 supplies some part in some quantity. By contrast, the tuple <S5> doesn't currently appear, though presumably it could; we can therefore assume that it's currently not the case that supplier S5 supplies any part in any quantity.

closure   1. (*Of a set of attributes*) The set of all attributes A such that the set {A} is functionally dependent on the given set. 2. (*Of a set of FDs*) The set of all FDs implied by the given set. 3. (*Of an algebra in general*) *See* Laws of Algebra, The. 4. (*Of relational algebra in particular*) The property that the result of every algebraic operation is a relation.

closure, transitive   *See* transitive closure.

CNF   Conjunctive normal form.

Codd, E. F.   The inventor of the relational model. See especially his papers (a) "Derivability, Redundancy, and Consistency of Relations Stored in Large Data Banks," IBM Research Report RJ599, August 19th, 1969 (the very first publication on the relational model); (b) "A Relational Model of Data for Large Shared Data Banks," *CACM 13,* No. 6, June 1970 (a revised and extended version of that first paper); and (c) "Relational Completeness of Data Base Sublanguages," in Randall Rustin (ed.), *Data Base Systems*: Courant Computer Science Symposia 6, Prentice-Hall (1972). The last of these papers in particular contains formal definitions of tuple calculus and Codd's original relational algebra, also of Codd's reduction algorithm, q.v.

Codd's reduction algorithm An algorithm for reducing an arbitrary tuple calculus expression to a semantically equivalent relational algebra expression. Among other things, the algorithm relies on the fact that the relational algebra operators projection and division are algebraic counterparts to the existential quantifier and the universal quantifier, respectively, of tuple calculus. *Note:* The existence of this algorithm suffices to show that Codd's original algebra is relationally complete (*see* relational completeness).

codomain *See* function.

coercion Implicit type conversion (usually best avoided).

collection (*Of an attribute, type, value, or variable*; *used as an adjective*) A special case of nonscalar, q.v., in which the user-visible component parts are usually required all to be of the same type; thus, for example, array and relation types might be regarded as collection types, but tuple types usually wouldn't be. The term is also used as a noun, in which case it serves as an abbreviation for any or all of collection type or collection value or collection variable (depending on context).

column 1. SQL analog of (a) an attribute of some relation or relvar, or (b) the bag or set of values of some attribute of some relation or relvar, or (c) the type of some attribute of some relation or relvar, or sometimes even (d) an attribute of some tuple or tuplevar or (e) the value of some attribute of some tuple or tuplevar or (f) the type of some attribute of some tuple or tuplevar (as the context demands). 2. More generally, a picture of an attribute (on paper, for example). *See also* cell; row; table.

common attribute An attribute that's common to two or more relations or relvars.

Examples: In the suppliers-and-parts database, (a) the pair <S#,S#> is a common attribute in relvars S and SP; (b) the pair <P#,P#> is a common attribute in relvars SP and P; and (c) the pair <CITY,CHAR> is a common attribute in relvars S and P. We might also say, more simply but less formally, just that (a) S# is a common attribute for relvars S and SP, (b) P# is a common attribute for relvars SP and P, and (c) CITY is a common attribute for relvars S and P.

commutative group *See* group (mathematics).

commutativity Let *Op* be a dyadic operator, and assume for definiteness that *Op* is expressed in infix style. Then *Op* is commutative if and only if, for all *x* and *y*, *x Op y* = *y Op x*.

Examples: In ordinary arithmetic, addition ("+") is commutative, because

$$x + y = y + x$$

for all *x* and *y*. In the same kind of way, UNION and JOIN are commutative in relational algebra (by contrast, MINUS is not). Likewise, OR and AND are commutative in logic (by contrast, IMPLIES is not). *Note*: It so happens that all of the commutative operators just mentioned are also associative, q.v. Examples of operators that are commutative but not associative include the logical operators NAND and NOR, q.v.

comparison A Boolean expression of the form (*exp1*) *theta* (*exp2*), where *exp1* and *exp2* are expressions of the same type *T* and *theta* is any comparison operator that makes sense for values of type *T* (certainly "=" or "≠", perhaps ">" also, and so on). *Note*: The parentheses enclosing *exp1* and *exp2* in the comparison might not be needed in practice.

compensating action / compensatory action An update performed automatically by the system in addition to some requested update, with the aim of avoiding some integrity violation that might otherwise occur.

Cascading a delete operation is a typical example. Such actions should be specified declaratively, and users should generally be aware of them; that is, users should generally know when their update requests are shorthand for some more extensive set of actions, for otherwise they might perceive an apparent violation of The Assignment Principle, q.v. *See also* multiple assignment; set level.

complement Let *r* be a relation with heading {*H*} and body {*b*}. Then the complement of *r* is the unique relation with heading {*H*} and body consisting of all tuples with heading {*H*} not appearing in {*b*}.

complement (*Set theory*) The complement—also known as the absolute complement—of a set *s* is the set of all elements not appearing in *s*. *Note*: The difference between sets *s1* and *s2*, in that order, is sometimes referred to as the relative complement of *s2* with respect to *s1* (*see* difference); thus, the absolute complement of *s* is in fact the relative complement of *s* with respect to the universal set, q.v. *See also* Boolean algebra (second definition).

complementarity 1. (*Logic*) The disjunction of a predicate and its negation is a tautology, q.v.; the conjunction of a predicate and its negation is a contradiction, q.v. 2. (*Set theory*) The union of a set and its complement is equal to the universal set, q.v.; the intersection of a set and its complement is equal to the empty set, q.v.

completeness (*Not to be confused with computational, relational, or truth functional completeness, q.v.*) That property of a formal system according to which, given a set *s* of sentences of the system, all sentences implied by those in *s* can be derived using the rules of inference of that system (i.e., all tautologies are theorems). *Contrast* soundness.

component (*Of a tuple*) *See* tuple component.

COMPOSE *See* composition.

composite attribute / compound attribute Deprecated terms for a combination of two or more attributes. The terms are deprecated because a "composite" or "compound" attribute isn't actually an attribute at all.

composite key / compound key A key consisting of two or more attributes.

Example: In the suppliers-and-parts database, SP is the only relvar with a composite key (namely, {S#,P#}).

composite predicate / compound predicate A predicate that involves at least one connective.

composite proposition / compound proposition A proposition that involves at least one connective.

composite statement / compound statement Syntactically, a statement that contains other statements nested inside itself.

Examples: Conventional IF, DO, WHILE, CASE statements; BEGIN . . . END . . . statement blocks; multiple assignment statements; and many others.

composition 1. (*Dyadic case*) Let *r1* and *r2* be relations. Then the composition of *r1* and *r2, r1* COMPOSE *r2,* is shorthand for (*r1* JOIN *r2*){*X*}, where {*X*} is all of the attributes of *r1* and *r2* apart from common ones. 2. (*N-adic case*) Let *r1, r2,..., rn* (*n* ≥ 0) be relations. Then the composition COMPOSE {*r1, r2,..., rn*} is shorthand for (JOIN {*r, r2,..., rn*}){*X*}, where {*X*} is all of the attributes of *r1, r2,..., rn* apart from ones common to at least two of those relations. *See also* tuple composition.

Example: *See* the example under recursive query.

computational completeness A language is computationally complete if and only if it supports the computation of all computable functions (where a computable function is a function that can be computed by a Turing machine in a finite number of steps).

Examples: C++; SQL; **Tutorial D**; and many others. Codd's original relational algebra is an example of a language that's not computationally complete.

conceptual modeling *See* semantic modeling.

conclusion In logic, that which a proof proves or an attempted proof attempts to prove.

conditional expression A logical expression, q.v.

conditional operator A read-only logical operator, q.v. (especially one of the connectives, q.v.).

conjunct A predicate that's ANDed with zero or more others.

conjunction 1. (*Dyadic case*) If p and q are predicates, their conjunction (p) AND (q) is a predicate also. Let (ip) AND (iq) be an invocation of that predicate (where ip and iq are invocations of p and q, respectively). Then that invocation (ip) AND (iq) evaluates to TRUE if and only if ip and iq both evaluate to TRUE. *Note*: The parentheses enclosing p and q in the conjunction might not be needed in practice. 2. (*N-adic case*) Let $p1$, $p2, \ldots , pn$ ($n \geq 0$) be predicates. Then the conjunction AND $\{p1,p2, \ldots ,pn\}$ is equivalent to the expression TRUE AND $(p1)$ AND $(p2)$ AND $\ldots$ AND (pn).

conjunctive normal form A predicate is in conjunctive normal form, CNF, if and only if it's of the form $(p1)$ AND $(p2)$ AND $\ldots$ AND (pn), where none of the conjuncts $(p1)$, $(p2)$, $\ldots$, (pn) involves any ANDs— more precisely, where each of the conjuncts $(p1)$, $(p2)$, $\ldots$, (pn) is a disjunction of literals (*see* literal, second definition).

connection trap A term used by some critics to refer to an alleged flaw in the relational model. Consider the expression (S JOIN P){S#,P#}. This expression denotes a relation, *r* say, that happens to contain the tuple <S2,P5> (because supplier S2 and part P5 are both located in Paris). Now, it obviously can't be inferred from this fact (at least, not validly) that supplier S2 supplies part P5—the predicate for *r* is "Supplier S# and part P# are located in the same city," not "Supplier S# supplies part P#." However, critics claim that users will nevertheless make that invalid inference, and hence that the relational model is flawed because it lets users fall into that trap. But it should be clear from the example that the flaw lies not with the model but with a failure on the part of those users (or those critics, perhaps) to understand the semantics of join. *Note*: As the example suggests, the term *connection trap* is typically regarded as an issue that arises in connection with join specifically (indeed, some writers even refer to it as the join trap for that reason); however, analogous issues can arise in connection with other operations also.

connective A read-only monadic or dyadic logical operator. There are exactly 20 connectives in two-valued logic, four monadic and 16 dyadic (corresponding directly to the four possible monadic and 16 possible dyadic truth tables). The connectives most frequently encountered in practice are NOT (negation), OR (disjunction), AND (conjunction), IMPLIES (implication), and EQUIV (equivalence); others include NAND, NOR, and XOR, q.v. *Note*: A variety of other symbols and keywords, some but not all of which are included in this dictionary, are also used to denote these connectives.

consequent *See* implication.

consistency Integrity, q.v. *Contrast* correctness.

consistent 1. (*Logic*) A set of predicates is consistent if and only if there exists at least one set of arguments that can be substituted for the parameters of those predicates such that every resulting proposition evaluates to TRUE. 2. (*Of a database*) Satisfying all defined integrity constraints.

Examples (*first definition*): Let the symbols *x, y,* and *z* denote integers. Then the predicates *x > y* and *y > z* form a consistent set, while the predicates *x > y, y > z,* and *z > x* do not.

constant A value, especially one that's named; not to be confused with a literal, q.v.

Example: *See* relation constant.

constraint An integrity constraint, q.v.

constraint inference The process of determining the constraints that apply to a given derived relvar or are satisfied by a given derived relation.

containment Generally, the relationship between a container and the things it contains; in particular, the relationship between a bag or set and its elements. *Contrast* inclusion.

contradiction A predicate whose every possible invocation is guaranteed to yield FALSE, regardless of what arguments are substituted for its parameters. *Note*: A contradiction in logic isn't quite the same thing as a contradiction in ordinary discourse. Loosely, we might say that (a) in ordinary discourse, a contradiction is something that implies that some proposition *p* and its negation NOT(*p*) are both true, while (b) in logic, by contrast, it's anything that's "always FALSE" (including, for example, the truth value FALSE itself). *Contrast* tautology.

Examples: Let *p1* be the predicate (actually a proposition) $2+2 = 5$; let *p2* be the predicate *x > x*, where *x* denotes an arbitrary integer; and let *p3* be the predicate (*p*) AND (NOT(*p*)), where *p* denotes an arbitrary proposition. Then *p1, p2,* and *p3* are all contradictions.

contrapositive The contrapositive of the implication IF (*p*) THEN (*q*) is the logically equivalent implication IF (NOT(*q*)) THEN (NOT (*p*)).

controlled redundancy Redundancy, q.v., is controlled if it does exist (and the user is aware of it), but the task of "propagating updates" to ensure that it never leads to any inconsistencies is managed by the DBMS, not the user. Uncontrolled redundancy can be a problem, but controlled redundancy shouldn't be. As a general rule, databases shouldn't include any uncontrolled redundancy.

correct *See* correctness.

correctness (*Of a database*) The property of truly reflecting the state of affairs that exists in the real world (see the example under relvar predicate for further discussion). *Contrast* consistency.

correlation name SQL term for either a tuple calculus range variable or the name of such a variable.

cover (*Of a set of FDs*) If $s1$ and $s2$ are sets of FDs, then $s2$ is a cover for $s1$ if and only if every FD implied by $s1$ is implied by $s2$. *Note*: Some writers use the term *cover* in a stronger sense, to mean a set of FDs that's equivalent to some given set (*see* equivalence).

cross join / cross product Cartesian product, q.v.

CWA The Closed World Assumption.

D

D Generic name used to refer to any language that conforms to the principles laid down by *The Third Manifesto*.

D_UNION *See* disjoint union.

data An encoded representation of propositions, assumed by convention to be true ones.

data definition operator An operator that either (a) defines some database object, such as a base relvar or a view or a snapshot or a constraint, or (b) deletes (drops) or updates such a definition; in other words, an operator that updates the catalog. *Note*: Dropping a definition effectively causes the corresponding object to be dropped as well (at least as far as the user is concerned), and is usually described in such terms. For example, **Tutorial D** provides an operator it calls DROP CONSTRAINT (not "drop constraint definition").

Examples: See the definitions of relvars S, P, and SP. Other examples could be (a) an operation to add an attribute to one of those relvars, or (b) an operation to define a constraint on those relvars, or (c) an operation to delete any of those definitions. (Strictly speaking, the first of these examples—"adding an attribute" to some relvar, say relvar S—has the effect of dropping the original relvar and introducing a new one with the same name, at the same time preserving, somehow, the information content of the original relvar. Details of how this effect might be achieved are beyond the scope of this dictionary.)

data independence The ability to change the physical or logical design of a database without having to make corresponding changes in the way the database is perceived by users. The terms *physical data independence* and *logical data independence* are used to refer to the two cases. Both involve having two sets of definitions and mappings between them, such that (a) if the physical design changes, physical data independence is preserved by changing the mapping from the physical design to the logical design, and (b) if the logical design changes, logical data independence is preserved by defining a mapping from the old logical design to the new one.

data manipulation operator Loosely, an operator that isn't a data definition operator. However, the distinction isn't hard and fast; in fact, it's hard to find an operator that doesn't, in the last analysis, "manipulate" data of some kind (unless it's a read-only operator, possibly; some writers might argue that update operators are the only ones that actually "manipulate" data). The term is probably best avoided.

data model 1. An abstract, self-contained, logical definition of the data structures, data operators, and so forth, that together make up the abstract machine with which users interact (*contrast* implementation). 2. A model of the persistent data of some particular enterprise (i.e., a logical database design).

Examples: For the second definition, any logical database design will suffice as an example. As for the first definition, the most obvious example is the relational model. There's a nice analogy that can help explain the difference between the two definitions, as follows: A data model in the first sense is like a programming language, whose constructs can be used to solve many specific problems but in and of themselves have no direct connection with any such specific problem; a data model in the second sense is like a specific program written in that language—it uses the facilities provided by the model, in the first sense of that term, to solve some specific problem. *Note*: We can sum up the distinction between a data model in the first sense and an implementation of that model by saying that the model is what the user has to know, while the implementation is what the user doesn't have to know.

data modeling Term sometimes used as a synonym for the logical database design process.

data sublanguage A language that provides database support for one or more distinct host languages, q.v., in which its statements can be embedded or from which they can be invoked.

Data Sublanguage ALPHA *See* ALPHA.

data type Type, q.v.

database Strictly, a database value, q.v.; more commonly used, in this dictionary in particular, to refer to what would more accurately be called a database variable, q.v. We assume throughout this dictionary that databases are always relational, barring explicit statements to the contrary. *Note*: The term *database* is also used in nonrelational contexts to mean a variety of other things: for example, a collection of data as physically stored. It's also used, all too frequently, to mean a DBMS, but this particular usage is strongly deprecated. (If we call the DBMS a database, what do we call the database?)

database constraint 1. (*"A"database constraint*) Formally, any constraint that isn't a type constraint (implying that constraints of all kinds apart from type constraints, including attribute and relvar constraints in particular, are just special cases); informally, any constraint that refers to two or more distinct relvars (also known as a multi-relvar constraint, q.v.). *Note*: These two definitions aren't meant to be equivalent in any sense—they refer to two distinct concepts. 2. (*"The" database constraint*) The logical AND of TRUE and all constraints, apart from type constraints, that apply to a given database (*the* database constraint—sometimes called the *total* database constraint—for the database in question). Note that it follows from this definition that every database is subject to at least one constraint: namely, the degenerate ("default") constraint TRUE. *See also* relvar constraint.

Examples: First, the key and foreign key constraints specified in the definition of the suppliers-and-parts database are all database constraints. Second, here are some more database constraints that might also apply to that database:

```
CONSTRAINT C1 IS_EMPTY
   ( S WHERE STATUS < 1 OR STATUS > 100 ) ;
/* status values must be in the */
/* range 1 to 100 inclusive      */

CONSTRAINT C2 IS_EMPTY
   ( P WHERE CITY = 'London' AND COLOR ≠ 'Red' ) ;
/* parts in London must be red */

CONSTRAINT C3 IS_EMPTY
   ( ( S JOIN SP )
     WHERE STATUS < 20 AND P# = P#('P6') ) ;
/* no supplier with status less */
/* than 20 can supply part P6    */
```

Finally, suppose for the sake of the example that the specified key and foreign key constraints, together with constraints C1–C3 above, are the only database constraints that apply to the suppliers-and-parts database. Then the logical AND of all of them and TRUE is "the" (total) database constraint for that database.

database design *See* logical database design; physical database design.

database management system The software system (the DBMS) that manages, and in particular handles all access to, some database or collection of databases. *Contrast* database.

database programming language A programming language that includes fully integrated ("native") database support. *Contrast* data sublanguage; host language.

Examples: **Tutorial D** might be regarded as a fully fledged database programming language, except that it currently includes no exception handling or I/O support. A similar remark applies to SQL; SQL is widely thought of as just a data sublanguage, q.v., but with the introduction into the 1992 version of the standard of such features as SQL variables, exception handling, IF, CASE, WHILE, CALL, RETURN, and assignment

(SET) statements, it too became a fully fledged database programming language (except that, like **Tutorial D**, it currently includes no I/O facilities).

database relvar *See* relvar.

database statistics Metadata, typically kept in the catalog, that might be helpful to the optimizer.

Examples: Relvar and attribute cardinalities; minimum, maximum, and average attribute values; attribute value frequencies; index selectivities; and so on.

database value Either the current or some possible "state" for some database; i.e., a collection of relations, those relations being possible values for the applicable relvars. Conceptually, therefore, a database value can be thought of as a set of propositions, those propositions corresponding to the tuples in the applicable relations. *Contrast* database variable.

Example: The relations (i.e., relation values) shown in Figure 1 constitute the "state" of the suppliers-and-parts database that happens to be current at some particular time. But if we were to look at that database at some different time, we would probably see a different state. In other words, the database is really a variable—a database variable, to be precise, meaning a variable whose values are database values. Moreover, the tuples in the relations that are the values of relvars S, P, and SP at any given time represent propositions—propositions that are assumed to be true at that time—so the database at the time in question can be thought of as a collection of true propositions.

database variable Loosely, a container for relvars; more accurately, a variable whose value at any given time is a database value. Strictly speaking, there's a logical difference, precisely analogous to that between relation values and relation variables, between database values and database variables. In other words, what we usually call a database is really a variable (typically a rather large one), and updating that database has the effect of replacing one value of that variable by another—where the values in question are database values and the variable in question is a database variable. More precisely, a database is a tuple variable, with one attribute (relation valued) for each relvar in the database in question. Note, therefore, that a database variable isn't really a set of relation variables, despite the fact that we often think of it that way informally. All of that being said, however, we bow to traditional usage elsewhere in this dictionary and use the term *database* to refer to both database values and database variables, relying on context to make clear which is intended. *See* database.

Example: *See* database value. As for the matter of a database really being a tuple variable, the suppliers-and-parts database in particular can be thought of as a tuple variable of the following tuple type:

```
TUPLE { S  RELATION { S# S#, SNAME NAME,
                      STATUS INTEGER, CITY CHAR },
         P  RELATION { P# P#, PNAME NAME, COLOR COLOR,
                      WEIGHT WEIGHT, CITY CHAR },
        SP RELATION { S# S#, P# P#, QTY QTY } }
```

DBMS Database management system; plural DBMSs.

dbvar A database variable, q.v. The term isn't much used.

DCO Domain check override.

De Morgan's Laws 1. (*Logic*) The negation of the disjunction of predicates p and q is equivalent to the conjunction of the negations of p and q; the negation of the conjunction of predicates p and q is equivalent to the disjunction of the negations of p and q. 2. (*Set theory*) The complement of the union of sets $s1$ and $s2$ is equal to the intersection of the complements of $s1$ and $s2$; the complement of the intersection of sets $s1$ and $s2$ is equal to the union of the complements of $s1$ and $s2$.

decidability That property of a formal system according to which, given an arbitrary sentence *s,* it can be determined whether or not *s* is a sentence of the system.

Examples: Propositional calculus is decidable; predicate calculus is not.

declared Term sometimes used as a synonym for defined or specified.

declared type 1. (*Of a value*) The type of the value in question. 2. (*Of a variable or an attribute*) The type specified when the variable or attribute in question is declared. 3. (*Of a read-only operator*) The type of the result, specified when the operator in question is declared. 4. (*Of an expression*) The type of the outermost operator involved in the expression in question. *Note*: The term *declared type* can safely be simplified to just *type* if inheritance is not supported. In the case of values, in fact, it's a slight fiction to refer to the type as a declared type anyway, since values as such aren't declared in the first place. Nevertheless, it's convenient, sometimes, to regard the type of a value as its declared type (it has the effect of simplifying certain other definitions).

decomposition Nonloss decomposition (unless the context demands otherwise).

deductive axiom Term occasionally used to mean a rule of inference.

DEE TABLE_DEE.

default value Let *A* be an attribute of relvar *R*. Barring explicit constraints to the contrary, then, a default value (default for short) can be declared for *A*; that value, *a* say, will appear as the *A* value in any tuple for which no other value is specified when the tuple in question is entered into *R*.

Example: Suppose attribute STATUS of relvar S has default value 10. Then the following INSERT might be valid, syntactically speaking:

```
INSERT S RELATION { TUPLE { S#     S#('S6'),
                            SNAME NAME('Lopez'),
                            CITY   'Madrid' } } ;
```

The relation that's actually inserted will look like this:

```
RELATION { TUPLE { S#     S#('S6'),
                   SNAME  NAME('Lopez'),
                   STATUS 10,
                   CITY   'Madrid' } }
```

Note: The two expressions in the foregoing example of the form
RELATION {TUPLE {. . .}} are relation selector invocations; each
denotes a relation containing just one tuple (i.e., a relation of cardinality
one). *See* selector.

deferred checking Checking an integrity constraint at some time
(typically commit time) later than the time when an update is performed
that might cause it to be violated. The relational model rejects deferred
checking as logically flawed. *Contrast* immediate checking.

deferred constraint An integrity constraint for which the checking is
deferred (*see* deferred checking). The relational model rejects deferred
constraints as logically flawed. *Contrast* immediate constraint.

degree The number n ($n \geq 0$) of attributes in a given heading, key, foreign
key, tuple, tuplevar, relation, or relvar.

Examples: The degrees of relvars S, P, and SP are four, five, and three,
respectively; the degrees of the corresponding keys are one, one, and two,
respectively.

DELETE Loosely, an operator that removes a given set of tuples from a
given relvar. It's shorthand for a certain relational assignment.

Example: The DELETE statement

```
DELETE S WHERE CITY = 'London' ;
```

is shorthand for the following relational assignment:

```
S := S WHERE NOT ( CITY = 'London' ) ;
```

DELETE rule A foreign key rule, q.v., that specifies the action to be taken by the DBMS if some tuple *t2* exists that contains a foreign key value referencing some tuple *t1* and—speaking rather loosely (*see* tuple level)—tuple *t1* is deleted.

denormalization Replacing a set of relvars *R1, R2, . . ., Rn* by their join *R*, such that for all *i* the projection of *R* on the attributes of *Ri* is guaranteed to be equal to *Ri* (*i* = 1, 2, . . ., *n*). Denormalization is usually done for performance reasons; however, it has the effect of increasing redundancy, q.v., thereby increasing (a) the amount of integrity checking that has to be done, or (b) the likelihood that certain update anomalies, q.v., will occur, or (c) both. It can also increase the complexity of certain queries. *Note*: Denormalization, at least to a level below 5NF, is always contraindicated from a logical point of view. Sometimes it can't be avoided, however, given the level of technology found in today's commercial products.

Example: A denormalization that might be applied to the suppliers-and-parts database would be to replace relvars S and SP by their join (SSP, say). Relvars S and SP could then be derived by projecting relvar SSP on the attributes of S and the attributes of SP, respectively.

dependant / dependent In an FD, the set of attributes on the right side. *Contrast* determinant.

Example: In the FD {S#,P#} → {QTY}, which is satisfied by relvar SP, {QTY} is the dependant and {S#,P#} is the determinant.

dependency An IND or JD or MVD or (especially) FD.

dependency preservation FD preservation, q.v.

dependency theory A body of theory, built on top of the relational model, that can be used to help with logical database design (though not limited to that purpose alone).

dereferencing *See* referencing.

derived relation Loosely, a relation defined in terms of others. More precisely, let *s* be a set of relations. Then relation *r* is derived from those in *s* if and only if it doesn't itself appear in *s* but can be obtained by means of some relational expression from those that do. That expression must be such that (a) every relational operand is a relation in *s* or one derived from those in *s* and (b) every relational operation is one of those defined in this dictionary, other than EXTEND, SUMMARIZE, and the read-only ("what if") form of UPDATE. *Contrast* base relation. *Note*: The purpose of the limitation on legal operators in this definition is to exclude the possibility of introducing some "completely new" relation (as it were) that's not otherwise derivable from *s*.

Example: Consider the expression S JOIN SP. If the current values of relvars S and SP are *s* and *sp,* respectively, this expression defines the derived relation that is the join of *s* and *sp*.

derived relvar A relvar defined in terms of others by means of some relational expression (in particular, a view or snapshot, q.v.). *Contrast* base relvar.

Examples: *See* snapshot; view.

descriptor A piece of metadata, describing, for example, a relvar or an attribute or a constraint.

designator An expression used in a predicate to designate some specific object (as opposed to a parameter). For example, in the predicate "The cardinality of relvar S is *n,*" the expression "relvar S" designates the relation that's the current value of the suppliers relvar (by contrast, *n* is a parameter).

determinant In an FD, the set of attributes on the left side. *Contrast* dependant.

Example: *See* dependant.

difference The difference between two relations *r1* and *r2* (in that order), *r1* MINUS *r2,* where *r1* and *r2* are of the same type *T,* is a relation of type *T* with body the set of all tuples *t* such that *t* appears in *r1* and not in *r2*. *Note*: The relational difference operator differs in certain respects from the mathematical or set theory operator of the same name, q.v. In fact, it's a special case of semidifference, q.v.

Example: The expression (S{CITY}) MINUS (P{CITY}) denotes the difference between the projections on {CITY} of the relations that are the current values of relvars S and P (in that order). That difference is a relation of type RELATION {CITY CHAR}. Moreover, if the current values of relvars S and P are *s* and *p,* respectively, the body of that relation consists of all tuples of the form <*c*> that appear in *s*{CITY} and not *p*{CITY}—meaning *c* is a current supplier city that isn't also a current part city. Note that the expression (S{CITY}) MINUS (P{CITY}) is semantically equivalent to the expression (S{CITY}) NOT MATCHING (P{CITY})—or the simpler expression (S{CITY}) NOT MATCHING P, come to that.

difference (bag theory) *See* bag.

difference (set theory) The set of all elements appearing in one given set and not in another. *See also* complement (set theory); *contrast* symmetric difference.

direct image A somewhat unsophisticated implementation style, found in most if not all of today's mainstream database products, in which what's physically stored is effectively just a direct image of what the user logically sees (i.e., relvars are stored as physical files, and tuples and attributes are stored as records and fields within those files).

direct proof *See* proof.

direct reasoning *See modus ponens.*

directed relationship A relationship, in the sense of the third definition of that term.

discernibility Distinguishability. *See* Principle of Identity of Indiscernibles, The.

disjoint (*Of a set of bags or sets*) Having no elements in common.

disjoint union A version of the relational union operator for which the operand relations are required to be disjoint, meaning they have no tuples in common. (This operation could obviously be generalized to apply to sets in general as well as relations in particular.)

Example: Consider the expression (S{CITY}) D_UNION (P{CITY}). If the current values of relvars S and P are as shown in Figure 1, this expression will cause a run-time error, because the operands aren't disjoint. If they were, however, the expression would then be semantically equivalent to (S{CITY}) UNION (P{CITY}).

disjunct A predicate that's ORed with zero or more others.

disjunction 1. (*Dyadic case*) If *p* and *q* are predicates, their disjunction (*p*) OR (*q*) is a predicate also. Let (*ip*) OR (*iq*) be an invocation of that predicate (where *ip* and *iq* are invocations of *p* and *q*, respectively). Then that invocation (*ip*) OR (*iq*) evaluates to TRUE if and only if at least one of *ip* and *iq* evaluates to TRUE. *Note*: The parentheses enclosing *p* and *q* in the disjunction might not be needed in practice. 2. (*N-adic case*) Let *p1*, *p2*, . . ., *pn* (*n* ≥ 0) be predicates. Then the disjunction OR {*p1,p2,. . .,pn*} is equivalent to the expression FALSE OR (*p1*) OR (*p2*) OR . . . OR (*pn*). *See also* inclusive OR.

disjunctive normal form A predicate is in disjunctive normal form, DNF, if and only if it's of the form (*p1*) OR (*p2*) OR . . . OR (*pn*), where none of the disjuncts (*p1*), (*p2*), . . ., (*pn*) involves any ORs—more precisely, where each of the disjuncts (*p1*), (*p2*), . . ., (*pn*) is a conjunction of literals (*see* literal, second definition).

DISTINCT *See* SELECT expression.

distributivity 1. Let operators *OpM* and *OpD* be monadic and dyadic, respectively, and assume for definiteness that *OpD* is expressed in infix style. Then *OpM* distributes over *OpD* if and only if, for all x and y, $OpM(x\ OpD\ y) = (OpM(x))\ OpD\ (OpM(y))$. 2. Let operators *OpC* and *OpD* both be dyadic, and assume for definiteness that they're expressed in infix style. Then *OpC* distributes over *OpD* if and only if, for all x, y, and z, $x\ OpC\ (y\ OpD\ z) = (x\ OpC\ y)\ OpD\ (x\ OpC\ z)$.

Examples: 1. (*Monadic over dyadic*) In ordinary arithmetic, nonnegative square root ("$\sqrt{}$") distributes over multiplication ("$*$"), because

$$\sqrt{(x * y)} = \sqrt{(x)} * \sqrt{(y)}$$

for all x and y. In the same kind of way, restriction distributes over UNION, INTERSECT, and MINUS in relational algebra.

2. (*Dyadic over dyadic*) Multiplication distributes over addition ("$+$"), because

$$x * (y + z) = (x * y) + (x * z)$$

for all x, y, and z. In the same kind of way, each of UNION and INTERSECT distributes over the other in relational algebra. Likewise, each of OR and AND distributes over the other in logic.

DIVIDEBY *See* division; Great Divide; Small Divide.

division Over the years several logically distinct relational division operators (i.e., operators that "divide" one relation by another) have been defined—so many, in fact, that it's probably better not to use the term at all, or at least to state explicitly in any given context which particular operator is intended. Two such operators are defined in this dictionary, the Great Divide and the Small Divide, q.v. *Note*: Earlier versions of **Tutorial D** supported both of these operators explicitly; the current version does not, because their functionality can be obtained by a variety of other means.

DK/NF Domain-key normal form.

DNF Disjunctive normal form.

domain Type. Earlier relational writings favored the term *domain*; more recent ones favor the term *type* instead.

domain (mathematics) *See* function; relation (mathematics).

domain calculus A form of relational calculus, semantically equivalent to tuple calculus, q.v., in which the range variables range over domains (types) instead of relations and thus denote values from those domains.

Example: Here's a domain calculus formulation of the query "Get supplier names for suppliers who supply at least one part" (*see* tuple calculus for a tuple calculus analog):

```
NX RANGES OVER { NAME } ;
SX RANGES OVER { S# }   ;
PX RANGES OVER { P# }   ;

NX WHERE
   EXISTS SX ( EXISTS PX ( S { S# SX, SNAME NX } AND
                           SP { S# SX, P# PX } ) )
```

In stilted English: "Get names NX where there exists a supplier number SX and there exists a part number PX such that a tuple with supplier number SX and supplier name NX appears in relvar S and a tuple with the same supplier number SX and part number PX appears in relvar SP."
As you can see, this particular example is somewhat clumsier than its tuple calculus counterpart (*see* tuple calculus), but there are also cases where the reverse is true.

domain check override An ad hoc and logically flawed—and therefore deprecated—mechanism for performing comparisons between values of different types. (It's flawed because it's based on a confusion over the logical difference between types and representations.)

domain-key normal form Relvar *R* is in domain-key normal form, DK/NF, if and only if every constraint that applies to *R* is implied by the attribute and key constraints that apply to *R*. (*Attribute-key normal form* would be a better name. In any case, the concept is mainly of academic interest, because relvars can easily be fully normalized— i.e., in 5NF or even 6NF—and still not be in DK/NF.)

Example: As noted under Boyce/Codd normal form, with the normal forms it's often more instructive to show a counterexample rather than an example per se. Suppose, therefore, that shipments satisfy a constraint to the effect that odd-numbered parts can be supplied only by odd-numbered suppliers and even-numbered parts only by even-numbered suppliers (the example is very contrived, of course, but it suffices for the purpose at hand). Then this constraint is clearly not implied by the attribute and key constraints that apply to relvar SP, and so SP isn't in DK/NF; yet it's certainly in 6NF.

domain relational calculus Domain calculus, q.v.

dot qualification In tuple calculus and languages based on it, a dot qualified name is an expression of the form *rx.A,* where *rx* is the name of a range variable and *A* is the name of an attribute of the relation *r* over which *rx* ranges. Such an expression serves as an attribute reference, q.v.; it denotes the value of attribute *A* (or possibly attribute *A* as such) within the particular tuple of *r* to which *rx* currently refers. Dot qualification is used for disambiguation purposes in tuple calculus—also in SQL—but not in domain calculus or relational algebra (these latter use attribute (re)naming and name scoping to achieve an equivalent effect).

Example: The following tuple calculus formulation of the query "Get suppliers who supply at least one part" makes use of two dot qualified names, SPX.S# and SX.S#:

```
SX   RANGES OVER { S } ;
SPX  RANGES OVER { SP } ;

SX WHERE EXISTS SPX ( SPX.S# = SX.S# )
```

Here for comparison is a relational algebra formulation of the same query:

```
S MATCHING SP
```

The "matching" here is done on the basis of attribute S# (since that attribute is the only one common to relvars S and SP).

double arrow *See* multivalued dependency.

double underlining A convention, illustrated in Figure 1, for marking attributes that participate in primary keys.

DRC Domain relational calculus.

drop *See* data definition operator.

dual 1. (*Logic*) The duals of AND, OR, TRUE, and FALSE are OR, AND, FALSE, and TRUE, respectively (NOT is its own dual). More generally, let x be a logical expression involving no connectives other than NOT, AND, and OR, and let y be obtained from x by replacing every occurrence of AND, OR, TRUE, and FALSE by its dual; then x and y are duals of each other. *Note*: Since every logical expression is equivalent to one involving no connectives other than NOT, AND, and OR, it follows that every logical expression has a dual. 2. (*Set theory*) The duals of intersection, union, the universal set, and the empty set are union, intersection, the empty set, and the universal set, respectively (complement is its own dual). More generally, let x be a set theory expression involving no operators other than complement, intersection, and union, and let y be obtained from x by replacing every occurrence of intersection, union, the universal set, and the empty set by its dual; then x and y are duals of each other. *Note*: Since every set theory expression is equivalent to one involving no operators other than complement, intersection, and union, it follows that every set theory expression has a dual. *See also* Duality Principle, The.

dual mode principle The principle that any relational operation that can be invoked interactively can also be invoked from an application program.

Duality Principle, The 1. (*Logic*) Let *x* and *y* be logical expressions such that *x* is the dual of *y*; then *x* is a tautology if and only if *y* is a tautology. 2. (*Set theory*) Let *x* and *y* be statements in set theory such that *x* is the dual of *y*; then *x* is a theorem if and only if *y* is a theorem.

Examples: De Morgan's Laws, q.v.

DUM TABLE_DUM.

duplicate Let *a1* and *a2* be appearances, q.v., in some context of values *v1* and *v2*, respectively. Then *a1* and *a2* are duplicates of each other if and only if *v1* and *v2* are equal (in other words, if and only if *v1* and *v2* are the very same value). Incidentally, it should be clear from this definition that the well known dictum to the effect that relations never contain duplicate tuples really means that no relation ever contains duplicate *appearances* of the *same* tuple—though we tend to stay with the less precise formulation in this dictionary for reasons of familiarity. Observe that since (a) relations never contain duplicate tuples and (b) every relational operation yields a relation, it follows that duplicate tuples (meaning, more precisely, redundant appearances of the same tuple) are eliminated, if necessary, whenever a relational operation is performed.

Examples (duplicate elimination): Given the sample values shown in Figure 1, the projection on {CITY} of the current value of relvar S has cardinality three, not five; similarly, the union of the projections on {CITY} of the current values of relvars S and P has cardinality four, not eleven. (Of the most familiar relational operators, projection and union are the only ones for which duplicate elimination is a concern. For the others—restriction, join, and so on—it's effectively a no op.)

duplicate elimination Term used ubiquitously to mean what would more accurately be called duplication elimination. *See* duplicate.

dyadic (*Of an operator*) Having exactly two operands; i.e., being defined in terms of exactly two parameters.

E

E/R Entity/relationship.

E/R diagram *See* entity/relationship diagram.

E/R model *See* entity/relationship model.

E/R modeling *See* entity/relationship modeling.

E-relation *See* RM/T.

element *See* bag; set.

embedded dependency A dependency satisfied by some projection of some relvar.

Example: Consider relvar CTXD, with attributes C (course), T (teacher), X (text), and D (days) and predicate "Teacher T spends D days with textbook X on course C." Let the sole key for that relvar be {C,T,X}. Assume also that for a given course, the set of teachers and the set of texts are quite independent of each other. Then CTXD is in 6NF—it can't be nonloss decomposed at all, other than trivially. Yet its projection on {C,T,X} satisfies the embedded multivalued dependencies {C} $\rightarrow\rightarrow$ {T} and {C} $\rightarrow\rightarrow$ {X}.

empty (*Of a bag or set*) Having no elements.

empty bag The bag with no elements (note that there's exactly one such); written (). (Of course, the empty bag () and the empty set {}, q.v., are logically indistinguishable.)

empty foreign key A foreign key of degree zero. *Note*: The corresponding candidate key in the referenced relvar will necessarily also be of degree zero, and the referential constraint will therefore be satisfied if and only if either (a) the referenced relvar is nonempty or (b) the referencing relvar is empty (or both).

empty heading The heading of degree zero (note that there's exactly one such).

empty key A key of degree zero. Note that a relvar with an empty key can't have any other keys in addition to the empty one, because of the irreducibility requirement on keys (*see* candidate key). Note too that such a relvar can't contain more than one tuple, because otherwise the key constraint would be violated. Declaring relvar R to have an empty key is thus a convenient way of imposing a cardinality constraint to the effect that R never contains more than one tuple.

empty range *See* existential quantifier; universal quantifier.

empty relation Given a relation type RELATION $\{H\}$, the relation of that type that contains no tuples at all. Note that there's exactly one empty relation for each relation type (and its cardinality is zero). *Contrast* universal relation.

Example: Suppose relvars S and P are both currently empty; that is, their current values s and p are both empty relations. Then s and p aren't equal, even though their bodies are equal, precisely because they're of different types (equivalently, because their headings aren't equal).

empty relvar A relvar whose current value is an empty relation.

empty restriction A restriction of a given relation r that contains no tuples (i.e., is equal to r WHERE FALSE); especially, a restriction of the form r WHERE c, where c is a contradiction, q.v.

Examples: Given the sample values in Figure 1, the expressions S WHERE STATUS = 25 and S WHERE STATUS > STATUS both denote empty restrictions (the second necessarily so, because STATUS > STATUS is a contradiction).

empty set The set with no elements (note that there's exactly one such); written {} or ø. All theorems, properties, definitions, etc., that apply to sets in general apply to the empty set in particular. For example, relation headings and bodies are both defined to be sets (of attributes and tuples, respectively), and so each is allowed to be the empty set in particular.

empty tuple The tuple of degree zero (note that there's exactly one such).

empty type A type with no values. This concept is of crucial importance if inheritance is supported but is perhaps of little use otherwise.

encapsulated Scalar. *Note*: The term is also used, especially in OO contexts, to refer to the physical bundling, or packaging, of code and data (or operator definitions and data representation definitions, to be more precise). But to use the term in this way is to mix model and implementation considerations; the user shouldn't care, and shouldn't need to care, whether or not code and data are physically bundled together.

entity A thing. *Note*: It's frequently suggested that there should be a one-to-one correspondence between "entities of interest" and tuples in base relvars. The suggestion is hard to sustain, however, given that the term *entities of interest* has no precise definition. (Of course, the same is true of the term *entity* itself, come to that.)

entity integrity The rule that attributes of primary keys in base relvars don't allow nulls. However, since (a) relvars, base or otherwise, don't necessarily have to have primary keys (*see* primary key) and (b) rules that apply to base relvars but not other kinds are more than a little suspect anyway (because they violate The Principle of Interchangeability), the entity integrity rule could be, and in fact has been, dropped without serious loss. We mention it here mainly for historical reasons. In any case, it refers to a concept, null, that is totally incompatible with the relational model; it would thus require major revision anyway before any suggestion that it be kept could be seriously entertained.

entity modeling *See* semantic modeling.

entity/relationship diagram A picture intended to explicate the logical design of a given database at a level of abstraction in which many details—in particular, details of the underlying types and almost all integrity constraints—are omitted.

entity/relationship model A set of conventions for drawing entity/relationship diagrams, q.v.

entity/relationship modeling Using the entity/relationship model, q.v., as a tool for assisting in the logical database design process.

EQ Same as EQUIV.

equality A truth valued operator; two values are equal if and only if they're the very same value. For example, the integer 3 is equal to the integer 3 and not to the integer 4, nor to any other integer (nor to anything else, either). More precisely, let T be a type; then the equality operator "=" for values of type T is defined as follows. Let $v1$ and $v2$ be two such values, and let Op be a read-only operator (other than "=" itself) with a parameter x of type T. Then $v1$ and $v2$ are equal (i.e., $v1 = v2$ evaluates to TRUE) if and only if, for all such operators Op, two successful invocations of Op that are identical in all respects except that the argument corresponding to x is $v1$ in one invocation and $v2$ in the other are indistinguishable in their effect. *Note*: The equality operator (which is—in fact, must be—defined for every type) is also known as identity. *See also* bag membership; duplicate; equivalence; identity, overloading; set; set membership; relation equality; tuple equality.

equijoin A theta join in which theta is "=".

EQUIV *See* equivalence.

equivalence 1. (*General*) Let x and y be elements of some set, and let that set be partitioned into a set of equivalence classes, q.v. Then x and y are equivalent (in symbols, $x \equiv y$) if and only if they're members of the same equivalence class. 2. (*Of sets of FDs*) Two sets of FDs are equivalent if and only if each is a cover for the other. *Note:* Any given set of FDs always has at least one equivalent set that's irreducible (*see* irreducible). 3. (*Logic, dyadic case*) If p and q are predicates, the equivalence (p) EQUIV (q) is a predicate also. Let (ip) EQUIV (iq) be an invocation of that predicate (where ip and iq are invocations of p and q, respectively). Then that invocation (ip) EQUIV (iq) evaluates to TRUE if and only if ip and iq both evaluate to TRUE or both evaluate to FALSE. (In other words, (p) EQUIV (q) is equivalent to (p) IMPLIES (q) AND (q) IMPLIES (p).) *See also* truth value of. *Note:* The parentheses enclosing p and q in the expression (p) EQUIV (q) might not be needed in practice. 4. (*Logic, n-adic case*) Let $p1, p2, \ldots, pn$ $(n \geq 0)$ be predicates. Then the equivalence EQUIV $\{p1,p2,\ldots,pn\}$ is a predicate also; and if $ip1, ip2, \ldots, ipn$ are invocations of $p1, p2, \ldots, pn$ (respectively), then the invocation EQUIV $\{ip1,ip2,\ldots,ipn\}$ returns TRUE if and only if exactly m of the invocations $ip1, ip2, \ldots, ipn$ return FALSE, where m is even. *Caveat:* This last definition is motivated by a desire to preserve associativity; to be specific, it has the property that the expressions EQUIV $\{p1,$EQUIV$\{p2,p3\}\}$, EQUIV $\{$EQUIV$\{p1,p2\},p3\}$, and EQUIV $\{p1,p2,p3\}$ are logically equivalent. (On the other hand, it also has the property that EQUIV $\{p1,p2,p3\}$ and NOT (XOR $\{p1,p2,p3\}$), as this latter expression is defined in this dictionary, are *not* equivalent. *See* exclusive OR.) It would be possible to come up with a different and possibly more intuitive definition, according to which the invocation EQUIV $\{ip1,ip2,\ldots,ipn\}$ returns TRUE if and only if all n of the invocations $ip1, ip2, \ldots, ipn$ return the same truth value. However, the two definitions are themselves clearly not equivalent (!), though they do coincide for $n = 2$; in other words, they define two logically distinct operators.

equivalence class A subset *ss* of some given set *s* with the property that the elements of *ss* are (a) all equivalent to one another, under some stated definition of equivalence, and (b) not equivalent to any other element of *s*, under that same definition of equivalence. (Note the relevance of this concept to relational grouping and summarization, q.v.; *see also* image relation.) For a more formal definition, *see* equivalence relation.

Examples: 1. Let *s* be the set of all positive integers, and define positive integers *x* and *y* to be equivalent if and only if they have the same number of digits in conventional decimal notation (no leading zeros). Then the subset of *s* containing all one-digit integers is an equivalence class under this definition of equivalence; so too are the subsets consisting of all two-digit integers, all three-digit integers, and so on. 2. Consider the set of parts currently represented by relvar P. Define two such parts to be equivalent if and only if they're of the same color. Then the set of all red parts currently represented in P is an equivalence class under this definition of equivalence; so too are the set of all blue parts, and the set of all yellow parts, and so on. 3. Consider the set of tuples in the current value of relvar SP. Define two such tuples to be equivalent if and only if they contain the same S# value. Then the set of all such tuples for supplier number S1 is an equivalence class under this definition of equivalence; so too are the set of all such tuples for supplier S2, and the set of all such tuples for supplier S3, and so on.

equivalence relation Let *r* be a binary relation. Then *r* is an equivalence relation if and only if it's reflexive, symmetric, and transitive, q.v. Further, let *x* be a value such that the tuple <*x,y*> appears in *r* for some *y*. Given that value *x*, then, the set of all such values *y* is an equivalence class with respect to *r*—namely, that specific equivalence class that corresponds to the given value *x* (*see* equivalence class). Observe that if *ry* is the set of all values *y* appearing in *r*, then every value in *ry* appears in exactly one equivalence class with respect to *r*—in other words, equivalence classes are pairwise disjoint, and together they partition the pertinent set of values.

essentiality Let *DM* be a data model in the first sense of that term (q.v.) and let *DS* be a data structure provided by *DM*. Let *dm* be a data model in the second sense of that term (created using the facilities of *DM*), and let *dm* include an occurrence *ds* of *DS*. Let *db* be a database conforming to *dm*. If removal from *db* of the data corresponding to *ds* would cause a loss of information from *db*, then *ds* is essential in *dm* (and, loosely, *DS* is essential in *DM*). For example, nonrelational systems typically provide numerous ways of representing information essentially, including (e.g.) pointers, record ordering, repeating groups, and so forth. *Note*: If data model *DM* supports *n* distinct data structures—in other words, if *DM* provides *n* distinct ways, essential or inessential, to represent information—then it's axiomatic that *DM* must also support *n* distinct sets of operators. However, there's nothing useful that can be done if $n > 1$ that can't be done if $n = 1$ (and $n = 1$ is the minimum, of course).

Example: For the relational model, we do have $n = 1$; that is, the relational model supports just one data structure, the relation itself, and that data structure is clearly essential, since if it were removed the model would be incapable of representing anything at all. However, since the relational model is in fact capable of representing absolutely any data whatsoever, any data model that supports relations in some shape or form as well as some additional data structure *DS* must be such that either relations are inessential or *DS* is. But if relations are inessential, then *DS* must be logically equivalent to relations!—in which case it could be argued that it's really *DS* that's inessential anyway, not relations. What's more, a data model that doesn't "support relations in some shape or form" is unlikely in the extreme; even SQL could be said to support relations if various SQL features—nulls, anonymous columns, duplicate rows, and so on—are avoided. Thus, for example, pointers (object IDs), bags, lists, and arrays could all be removed from the so called object model without any loss of representational power. Indeed, the fact that they're not removed is prima facie evidence that "the object model" fails to distinguish properly between model and implementation issues.

EXCEPT SQL analog of MINUS.

exclusive OR 1. (*Dyadic case*) If p and q are predicates, their "exclusive OR" (p) XOR (q) is a predicate also. Let (ip) XOR (iq) be an invocation of that predicate (where ip and iq are invocations of p and q, respectively). Then that invocation (ip) XOR (iq) evaluates to TRUE if and only if exactly one of ip and iq evaluates to TRUE. (In other words, (p) XOR (q) is equivalent to NOT((p) EQUIV (q)).) *Note*: The parentheses enclosing p and q in the expression (p) XOR (q) might not be needed in practice. 2. (*N-adic case*) Let $p1, p2, \ldots, pn$ ($n \geq 0$) be predicates. Then the "exclusive OR" XOR $\{p1,p2,\ldots,pn\}$ is a predicate also; and if $ip1, ip2, \ldots, ipn$ are invocations of $p1, p2, \ldots, pn$ (respectively), then the invocation XOR $\{ip1,ip2,\ldots,ipn\}$ returns TRUE if and only if exactly m of the invocations $ip1, ip2, \ldots, ipn$ return TRUE, where m is odd. *Caveat*: This latter definition is motivated by a desire to preserve associativity; to be specific, it has the property that the expressions XOR $\{p1,\text{XOR}\{p2,p3\}\}$, XOR $\{\text{XOR}\{p1,p2\},p3\}$, and XOR $\{p1,p2,p3\}$ are logically equivalent. (On the other hand, it also has the property that XOR $\{p1,p2,p3\}$ and NOT (EQUIV $\{p1,p2,p3\}$), as this latter expression is defined in this dictionary, are *not* equivalent. *See* equivalence.) It would be possible to come up with a different and possibly more intuitive definition, according to which the invocation XOR $\{ip1,ip2,\ldots,ipn\}$ returns TRUE if and only if exactly one of the invocations $ip1, ip2, \ldots, ipn$ returns TRUE. However, the two definitions are themselves clearly not equivalent, though they do coincide for $n = 2$; in other words, they define two logically distinct operators.

existential quantifier Let $p(x)$ be a predicate with a parameter x; then EXISTS x ($p(x)$) is a predicate, and it means "There exists at least one argument v that can replace the parameter x such that $p(v)$ is true." In this example, EXISTS x is an existential quantifier, and x is an existentially quantified bound variable, q.v. *Note*: Some writers refer to EXISTS by itself as the quantifier; the literature is not consistent on this point. More important, note that if $v1, v2, \ldots, vn$ are all of the possible arguments in the foregoing example, then EXISTS x $(p(x))$ is equivalent to $(p(v1))$ OR $(p(v2))$ OR . . . OR $(p(vn))$ OR FALSE. Observe in particular that this expression evaluates to FALSE if $n = 0$ (i.e., if the bound variable x ranges over an empty set). Observe further that the expression EXISTS x $(p(x))$ is logically equivalent to the expression NOT (FORALL x (NOT $(p(x))$))). *See also* UNIQUE; *contrast* universal quantifier.

Examples: *See* bound variable; domain calculus; free variable; tuple calculus; and elsewhere.

EXISTS *See* existential quantifier. In the literature, EXISTS is often represented by a backward E, thus: ∃.

expanded Cartesian product *See* Cartesian product.

expressible relation Any relation that, given a particular set of relations, is either contained in that set or can be derived from those that are (*see* derived relation).

expressible relvar Any relvar that, given a particular set of relvars, is either contained in that set or can be derived from those that are (*see* derived relvar).

expression In a programming language, a read-only operator invocation; a construct that denotes a value; hence, a rule for computing, or determining, the value in question. Every expression is of some type—namely, the type of the value it denotes. Note that constant and variable names (i.e., variable references, q.v.) are both considered to be read-only operator invocations and hence both constitute legal expressions. *Contrast* statement.

Examples: X+Y is an expression; in fact, it's an invocation of the "+" operator, and it denotes the value that's the sum of the current values of the variables X and Y. By contrast,

```
Z := X + Y ;
```

is a statement; it assigns the value denoted by the expression X+Y on the right side to the variable Z referenced on the left side. *Note*: In both of the foregoing examples, X and Y are variable references and thus themselves expressions in turn.

expression transformation Transforming a given expression into another, semantically equivalent expression. The process applies to relational expressions in particular, where it's sometimes called "query rewrite." Query rewrite is typically done for performance reasons; it can be done either by the user or, much more importantly, by the system (*see* optimizer). *Note*: The term *query rewrite* is also used in certain commercial products with a somewhat more limited meaning. *Caveat lector.*

Example: The relational expression (*r* WHERE *br*) JOIN (*s* WHERE *bs*) is semantically equivalent to the relational expression (*r* JOIN *s*) WHERE (*br*) AND (*bs*); therefore, either expression can be transformed into the other. Transforming the second into the first is likely to be advantageous from a performance standpoint, because the first means doing the restrictions before the join; thus, it's likely that the input relations to the join will be smaller and the output will be smaller too. In fact, this transformation could make the difference between keeping the result of the join in memory and having to spill it out on to the disk.

EXTEND *See* extension.

extended Cartesian product *See* Cartesian product.

Extensible Markup Language *See* XML.

extension 1. (*Relational algebra*) Let *r* be a relation. Then the extension EXTEND *r* ADD (*exp* AS *X*) is a relation with (a) heading the heading of *r* extended with attribute *X*, and (b) body consisting of all tuples *t* such that *t* is a tuple of *r* extended with a value for attribute *X* that's computed by evaluating the expression *exp* on that tuple of *r*. Relation *r* must not have an attribute called *X*, and *exp* must not refer to *X*. *See also* tuple extension.

2. (*Predicate*) Let *p* be a predicate; then the extension of *p* consists of all full instantiations of *p* (i.e., all propositions that can be derived from *p* by full instantiation) that evaluate to TRUE. 3. (*Relation*) Following on from the previous definition, let *r* be a relation. Then the heading of *r* can be regarded as representing a predicate (*see* relation predicate), and the body of *r* can be regarded as representing the extension of that predicate. Hence, the term *extension* is also sometimes used to refer to the body of a relation. *Contrast* intension. 4. (*Set theory*) *See* axiom of extension.

Example (*first definition only*): The following expression denotes an extension of the relation that's the current value of relvar P:

```
EXTEND P ADD ( WEIGHT * 454 AS GMWT )
```

That extension is a relation just like the current value of relvar P, except that it has an additional attribute GMWT ("gram weight"), whose value in any given tuple is 454 times the WEIGHT value in that same tuple. Note that relvar P per se remains unaltered in the database—EXTEND isn't like ALTER TABLE in SQL, it's just a read-only operator that (like restrict, for example) takes a certain relation as input and returns another as output. Further examples are given under summarization.

external predicate The relvar predicate for a given relvar. *Contrast* internal predicate. *Note*: Since this latter term is deprecated, the term *external predicate* is deprecated (somewhat) as well.

F

FALSE *See* BOOLEAN.

FD Functional dependency.

FD implied by a superkey The FD $A \rightarrow B$ is implied by a superkey if and only if A is a superkey for the pertinent relvar.

FD preservation Decomposing a relvar R into its projections $R1$, $R2, \ldots, Rn$ in such a way that FDs are preserved—that is, every FD satisfied by R is implied by those satisfied by $R1, R2, \ldots, Rn$. $R1$, $R2, \ldots, Rn$ here are said to be independent projections. *Note*: Projections that aren't independent are said to be interdependent, not dependent. *See also* atomic relvar.

Example: Suppose relvar S satisfies the additional FD {CITY} $\rightarrow$ {STATUS}; i.e., the status for a given supplier is a function of that supplier's location. Then replacing S by its projections on {S#,SNAME,CITY} and {CITY,STATUS} preserves FDs, because every FD satisfied by S is either satisfied by one of the two projections or is implied by those that are. By contrast, suppose S is replaced by its projections on {S#,SNAME,CITY} and {S#,STATUS} instead. Now the FD {CITY} $\rightarrow$ {STATUS} isn't implied by the FDs satisfied by those projections (even though the decomposition is nonloss). One practical consequence is that updates to either of the two projections must now be monitored (either by the DBMS or—more likely in current practice—by some application) to ensure that the FD {CITY} $\rightarrow$ {STATUS} continues to be satisfied; for example, consider what's involved in moving supplier S1 from London to Paris. In other words, the two projections aren't independent in this latter decomposition but are, rather, interdependent. Given the level of technology found in today's commercial products, therefore, it's generally preferable to perform decomposition in such a way as to preserve FDs—i.e., to decompose into independent projections—whenever possible.

field Term sometimes used to mean a column, in any of the possible senses of that term. All such uses are deprecated, however; the term is better reserved for an operating system or even physical level construct.

field (mathematics) An algebra, q.v., for which the operators "+" and "*" have all of the properties (commutativity, associativity, etc.) that addition and multiplication of real numbers have; equivalently, a formal system that obeys all of The Laws of Algebra, q.v.

fifth normal form Relvar R is in fifth normal form, 5NF, if and only if every nontrivial JD satisfied by R is implied by the superkeys of R; equivalently, if and only if every nontrivial JD $\Diamond\{A1,A2,...,An\}$ satisfied by R is such that (a) each of $A1, A2, ..., An$ is a superkey for R and (b) the keys of R can be ordered in such a way that each pair of adjacent keys in that ordering is included in some Ai, $1 \le i \le n$. Every 5NF relvar is in 4NF. *Note*: 5NF is "the" normal form with respect to JDs. Also, although being in 5NF clearly doesn't preclude being in 6NF as well, the term *5NF* is often used loosely to refer to a relvar that's in 5NF and not in 6NF. Observe that relvar R is certainly in 5NF if either (a) it's in 3NF and it has no composite keys or (b) it's in BCNF and it has at least one nonkey attribute.

Example: As noted under Boyce/Codd normal form, with the normal forms it's often more instructive to show a counterexample rather than an example per se. Consider, therefore, relvar SPJ, with attributes S# (supplier number), P# (part number), and J# (project number), and predicate "Supplier S# supplies part P# to project J#." Let that relvar be all key (i.e., subject to the key constraint KEY{S#,P#,J#}). Let it also be subject to the constraint that if (a) supplier Sx supplies part Py and (b) part Py is supplied to project Jz and (c) project Jz is supplied by supplier Sx, then (d) supplier Sx supplies part Py to project Jz. Then SPJ is equal to the join of its projections on {S#,P#}, {P#,J#}, and {J#,S#}—i.e., it satisfies the JD ⟡ {{S#,P#},{P#,J#},{J#,S#}}—and so it can be nonloss decomposed into those three projections. Since that JD is neither trivial nor implied by the sole superkey (namely, the entire heading), relvar SPJ isn't in 5NF, though it is in 4NF. We remark that relvar SPJ (a) is in 3NF but has a composite key and (b) is in fact in BCNF but has no nonkey attributes.

file Term sometimes used to mean a table, in any of the possible senses of that term, or even a relation or relvar. All such uses are deprecated, however; the term is better reserved for an operating system or even physical level construct.

First Great Blunder, The Equating types and either relations or relvars. *See* type.

first normal form Normalized. All relvars are in first normal form, 1NF, by definition; that is, the terms *1NF* and *normalized,* applied to a relvar, mean the same thing (*see* normalized for further explanation). It follows that a "table," in a language like SQL, can be considered to be in 1NF if and only if it's a direct and faithful representation of some relvar, where *direct and faithful* means among other things that every row-and-column intersection (i.e., every cell, q.v.) in that table contains exactly one value of the applicable type, nothing more and nothing less. (The value in question can be arbitrarily complex—it can even be a table—but, to repeat, there must be exactly one such, and it must be of the applicable type.) In particular, therefore, a table isn't in first normal form if it contains any repeating groups, q.v. This fact accounts for the usual informal characterization of first normal form as meaning simply *no repeating groups*. *Note*: Although being in 1NF clearly doesn't preclude being in 2NF as well, the term *1NF* is often used loosely to refer to a relvar that's in 1NF only and not in any higher normal form.

first order logic A form of predicate logic in which the sets over which variables range aren't allowed to contain predicates. *Contrast* second order logic. *Note*: Propositional logic, q.v., might be regarded as a "zeroth order" logic, because it has no variables (and its variables thus don't range over anything at all).

flat relation The idea that "relations are flat" is a popular misconception (and the phrase "flat relation" is strongly deprecated). *See* table.

FORALL *See* universal quantifier. In the literature, FORALL is often represented by an upside down A, thus: $\forall$.

foreign key Let $R1$ and $R2$ be relvars, not necessarily distinct, and let K be a key for $R1$. Let FK be a subset of the heading of $R2$ such that there exists a possibly empty sequence of attribute renamings on $R1$ that maps K into K' (say), where K' and FK contain exactly the same attributes. Further, let $R2$ and $R1$ be subject to the constraint that, at all times, every tuple $t2$ in $R2$ has an FK value that's the K' value for some (necessarily unique) tuple $t1$ in $R1$ at the time in question. Then FK is a foreign key, the associated constraint is a referential constraint, and $R2$ and $R1$ are the referencing relvar and the corresponding referenced relvar, respectively, for that constraint. Also, K (not K') is referred to, sometimes, as the referenced key or target key. *Note*: The referencing and referenced terminology carries over to tuples in the obvious way; that is, tuples $t2$ and $t1$ from the foregoing discussion are a referencing tuple and the corresponding referenced tuple, respectively. A referenced tuple is also sometimes called a target tuple.

Examples: In relvar SP, {S#} and {P#} are foreign keys corresponding to the keys {S#} and {P#} in relvars S and P, respectively. They might be specified as follows:

```
VAR SP BASE RELATION
  { S# S#, P# P#, QTY QTY }
    KEY { S#, P# }
```

```
    FOREIGN KEY { S# } REFERENCES S
    FOREIGN KEY { P# } REFERENCES P ;
```

Here by contrast is an example in which some attribute renaming is required:

```
VAR EMP BASE RELATION
   { E# E#, ..., M# E#, ... }
     KEY { E# }
     FOREIGN KEY { M# } REFERENCES
             ( EMP { E# } ) RENAME ( E# AS M# ) ;
```

Attribute M# here denotes the employee number of the manager of the employee identified by E# (the referencing relvar and the referenced relvar in this example are one and the same). Thus, for example, the EMP tuple for employee E3 might contain an M# value of E2, which constitutes a reference to the EMP tuple for employee E2.

Note that there's no requirement that the key in the referenced relvar that corresponds to a given foreign key be a primary key specifically. Nor is there a requirement that the referencing relvar and the referenced relvar be base relvars specifically.

foreign key constraint A referential constraint, q.v.

foreign key rule A rule specifying the action to be taken by the DBMS— typically but not necessarily a compensating action, q.v.—to ensure that updates affecting the foreign key in question don't violate the associated foreign key constraint.

formal Having to do with form rather than content (though the term also carries connotations of precision, and its opposite, informal, is often used as if it were a synonym for intuitive). By way of example, consider the expression (actually a functional dependency) $\{S\#\} \rightarrow \{CITY\}$. This FD is a formal statement, and it has a certain precise (formal!) significance: namely, that whenever two tuples in relvar S have the same S# value, they also have the same CITY value. By contrast, the real world constraint that this FD is supposed to represent looks something like this: *Each supplier* *is located in just one city.* This latter statement is an example of what some would call a business rule, q.v., and it's quite informal (note in particular that it relies on the concepts "supplier," "city," and "is located in," none of which is formally defined).

formal operand A parameter, q.v.

formal system A logical system, q.v.

formula Same as well-formed formula.

fourth normal form Relvar R is in fourth normal form, 4NF, if and only if every nontrivial MVD satisfied by R is implied by some superkey of R; equivalently, if and only if for every nontrivial MVD $A \rightarrow\rightarrow B$ satisfied by R, A is a superkey for R (and the MVD $A \rightarrow\rightarrow B$ in fact degenerates to the FD $A \rightarrow B$). Every 4NF relvar is in BCNF. *Note*: 4NF is "the" normal form with respect to MVDs. Also, although being in 4NF clearly doesn't preclude being in the next higher normal form (5NF) as well, the term *4NF* is often used loosely to refer to a relvar that's in 4NF and not in 5NF. In any case, fourth normal form as such is no longer very important (BCNF, 5NF, and 6NF being the normal forms of most practical significance); we mention it here mainly for historical reasons.

Example: As noted under Boyce/Codd normal form, with the normal forms it's often more instructive to show a counterexample rather than an example per se. Consider, therefore, relvar CTX, with attributes C (course), T (teacher), and X (text), and predicate "Course C can be taught by teacher T and uses text X as a textbook." Let that relvar be all key (i.e., subject to the key constraint KEY{C,T,X}). Assume also that for a given course, the set of teachers and the set of texts are quite independent of each other. Then CTX is equal to the join of its projections on {C,T} and {C,X}—i.e., it satisfies the MVDs {C} $\rightarrow\rightarrow$ {T} and {C} $\rightarrow\rightarrow$ {X}— and so it can be nonloss decomposed into those two projections. Since those MVDs are neither trivial nor implied by the sole superkey (namely, the entire heading), relvar CTX isn't in 4NF, though it is in BCNF.

free variable In logic, a variable—more precisely, an occurrence of a variable reference within some predicate—that isn't bound; in other words, a parameter. (The term *variable* is used here in the sense of logic, not in the programming language sense.) *Contrast* bound variable.

Examples: Let the symbols x and y denote integers. Then the following expressions are both predicates, and x appears as a free variable in each of them:

```
x < 7
```

```
EXISTS y ( y > 3 ) AND x < 7
```

The first predicate is self-explanatory. The second is a little more complicated because it involves a quantified subexpression (in which y appears, twice, as a bound variable) as well as the free variable x.

Turning to a database example, the following is a query ("Get suppliers who supply at least one part") on the suppliers-and-parts database, expressed in tuple calculus:

```
S WHERE EXISTS SP ( SP.S# = S.S# )
```

The Boolean expression following the keyword WHERE here is a predicate, and the reference to S in that predicate is free (by contrast, the references to SP are bound). Note, however, that in this particular example the symbols S and SP denote not only variables in the sense of logic but also variables in the conventional programming language sense—but that's because we've indulged in a certain sleight of hand, as it were. Here's an extended version of the same example that should help clarify matters:

```
SX   RANGES OVER { S } ;
SPX RANGES OVER { SP } ;

SX WHERE EXISTS SPX ( SPX.S# = SX.S# )
```

Here SX and SPX have been explicitly declared as variables in the sense of logic, ranging over (the current values of) relvars S and SP, respectively.

Now it's the reference to SX that's free and the references to SPX that are bound (in the predicate following the keyword WHERE in both cases). *Note*: Let *VR* be a variable reference that occurs prior to the WHERE clause—i.e., within the proto tuple, q.v.—in some tuple calculus expression. If *VR* also occurs in the predicate in that WHERE clause (which it often but not invariably will), then it must be free, not bound, in that predicate.

full FD Old fashioned and somewhat deprecated (because slightly inappropriate) term for a left irreducible FD.

full instantiation *See* instantiation.

fully dependent Old fashioned and somewhat deprecated (because slightly inappropriate) term for irreducibly dependent.

fully normalized A database is fully normalized if and only if every relvar it contains is in at least 5NF (i.e., if and only if every such relvar is fully normalized in turn).

function 1. (*Mathematics*) Given two sets, not necessarily distinct, a rule—also known as a map or mapping—pairing each element of the first set (the domain) with exactly one element of the second set (the codomain); equivalently, the set of ordered pairs $<x,y>$ that constitutes that pairing. The unique element y of the codomain corresponding to element x of the domain is the image of x under the specified function, and the set of all such images is the range of that function. Note that the range is a subset (often a proper subset) of the codomain, and the function can be regarded as a directed relationship—in fact, a many-to-one correspondence, in the strict sense of that term—from the domain to the range. Note too that a function is a special case of a binary relation. *See also* partial function; total function. 2. (*Programming languages*) A read-only operator (sometimes more specifically one denoted by an identifier such as DIV instead of by a special symbol such as "/"). Note, however, that the programming language construct denoted by this term is precisely a function in the mathematical sense; thus, there's really just one concept here, not two. Note also that nothing in the definition requires the domain and codomain to be sets of scalars; thus, a read-only operator could be defined in terms of, say, three parameters, in which case the domain would consist of a set of triples. A similar remark applies to the codomain.

Example: Let f be the rule that maps nonnegative integers x to their squares x^2. Then we can say that f is a function with (a) domain and codomain both the set of all nonnegative integers and (b) range that subset of the codomain consisting only of perfect squares.

functional dependency An expression—actually a proposition—of the form $A \rightarrow B$, where the determinant A and the dependant B are both subsets of the heading of the same relvar R, and the expression overall is read as "B is functionally dependent on A," or "A functionally determines B," or, more simply, just "A arrow B." Relvar R satisfies the functional dependency (FD) $A \rightarrow B$—equivalently, that FD holds in relvar R—if and only if, in every relation that's a legal value for R, whenever two tuples have the same value for A, they also have the same value for B (*see* function). *Note*: Functional dependency is also known as functional dependence. Observe that A and B in the FD $A \rightarrow B$ are, specifically, sets of attributes; informally, however, it's common (though strictly incorrect) to speak of the attributes in B as if those attributes per se, instead of the set B that contains those attributes, were functionally dependent on A. Likewise, it's common (though strictly incorrect) to speak of the attributes in A as if B were functionally dependent on those attributes per se, instead of on the set A that contains those attributes. Note finally that from a formal point of view, an FD $A \rightarrow B$ is just a proposition that, by definition, can be either satisfied or not (i.e., can evaluate to either TRUE or FALSE); informally, however, it's common to define $A \rightarrow B$ to be an FD only if it's actually satisfied by the pertinent relvar. But that definition leaves no way of saying that a given relvar fails to satisfy, or violates, some FD (because, by that definition, an FD that isn't satisfied isn't an FD!).

Example: Suppose for the sake of the example that relvar SP has an additional attribute CITY, representing the city of the applicable supplier. Then that revised version of SP satisfies the FD $\{S\#\} \rightarrow \{CITY\}$. Note in particular in this example that the determinant isn't a key of the relvar concerned. (By definition, every relvar R always satisfies all possible FDs of the form $K \rightarrow X$, where K is a key—or, more generally, a superkey—for R and X is an arbitrary subset of the heading of R. In other words, there are always "arrows out of superkeys," and it's "arrows not out of superkeys" that are, in a sense, the interesting ones.)

functionally dependent *See* functional dependency.

functionally determines *See* functional dependency.

G

generated type *See* type generator.

generic operator An operator that's available in connection with every type that can be produced by invocation of some given type generator, q.v. For example, the operators of the relational algebra are generic: they're available for relations of every type that can be produced by invocation of the relation type generator—in other words, for relations of all possible types, and hence for all relations.

generic polymorphism The kind of polymorphism exhibited by a generic operator, q.v.

Golden Rule, The The rule that no database is ever allowed to violate its own total database constraint. It follows that no relvar is ever allowed to violate its own total relvar constraint either, a fortiori. *Note*: This latter, weaker requirement is often referred to as **The Golden Rule** as well, though strictly speaking it's merely a logical consequence of **The Golden Rule** proper.

Great Blunder A somewhat contentious term that has been used in connection with certain violations of relational principles. *See* First Great Blunder, The; Second Great Blunder, The.

Great Divide One of the many relational division operators that have been defined over the years (*see* division). Let relations $r1$, $r2$, $r3$ and $r4$ be such that (a) $r1$ and $r2$ have no attribute names in common; (b) attributes with the same name in $r1$ and $r3$ are of the same type, and so are attributes with the same name in $r3$ and $r4$, and so are attributes with the same name in $r4$ and $r2$ (in other words, $r1$ and $r3$ are joinable, and so are $r3$ and $r4$, and so are $r4$ and $r2$); (c) the sets $\{X\}$, $\{Y\}$, and $\{Z\}$ are the common attributes of $r1$ and $r3$, of $r3$ and $r4$, and of $r4$ and $r2$, respectively; and (d) the sets $\{X\}$ and $\{Y\}$ are disjoint, and so are the sets $\{Y\}$ and $\{Z\}$. Then the division $r1$ DIVIDEBY $r2$ PER $(r3,r4)$—where $r1$ is the dividend, $r2$ is the divisor, and r3 and r4 are the "mediators"—is a relation with heading the set theory union of the headings of *r1* and *r2* and with body defined as follows: Tuple *t* appears in that body if and only if it appears in *r1* JOIN *r2* and a tuple <*x,y*> with *x* equal to the *X* value in *t* appears in *r3*{*X,Y*} for all tuples <*y,z*> in *r4*{*Y,Z*} with *z* equal to the *Z* value in *t*. In other words, the expression *r1* DIVIDEBY *r2* PER (*r3,r4*) is semantically equivalent to the expression (*r1* JOIN *r2*) NOT MATCHING ((*r1*{*X*} JOIN *r4*{*Y,Z*}) NOT MATCHING *r3*). *Contrast* Small Divide.

Examples: Suppose we're given a revised version of the suppliers-and-parts database—a version that's both extended and simplified, compared to our usual running example, and looks like this:

```
S    { S# }
SP   { S#, P# }
PJ   { P#, J# }
J    { J# }
```

Relvar J here represents projects (J# stands for project number), and relvar PJ indicates which parts are used in which projects. Then the division S DIVIDEBY J PER (SP,PJ) yields a relation with heading {S#,J#} and body consisting of all possible tuples of the form <*s#,j#*> (where *s#* is an S# value currently appearing in relvar S, *j#* is a J# value currently appearing in relvar J, and supplier *s#* supplies all parts used in project *j#*), and no other tuples. The expression is semantically equivalent to this one:

```
( S JOIN J ) NOT MATCHING
     ( ( S JOIN PJ ) NOT MATCHING SP )
```

An equivalent tuple calculus formulation is

```
SX   RANGES OVER { S }  ;
SPX  RANGES OVER { SP } ;
PJX  RANGES OVER { PJ } ;
JX   RANGES OVER { J }  ;


( SX, JX ) WHERE FORALL PJX ( EXISTS SPX
```

```
            (  SX.S#  =  SPX.S#  AND
                SPX.P#  =  PJX.P#  AND
                PJX.J#  =  JX.J#  )  )
```

An equivalent **Tutorial D** formulation is

```
  (  S  JOIN  J  )  WHERE  !!PJ  ⊆  !!SP
```

(*see* image relation).

Incidentally, observe what happens if the operands to the foregoing division are switched around, thus: J DIVIDEBY S PER (PJ,SP). This expression yields a relation with heading {J#,S#} and body consisting of all possible tuples of the form <*j#,s#*> (where *j#* is a J# value currently appearing in relvar J, *s#* is an S# value currently appearing in relvar S, and project *j#* uses all parts supplied by supplier *s#*), and no other tuples. An equivalent **Tutorial D** formulation is

```
  (  J  JOIN  S  )  WHERE  !!SP  ⊆  !!PJ
```

greater-than join A theta join in which theta is ">".

GROUP See grouping.

group Term sometimes used in connection with the grouping operator, q.v. Let *r* be a relation, let {*X*} be a subset of the heading of *r*, and let the projection *r*{*X*} have cardinality *n* ($n \geq 0$). Then *r* can be partitioned into exactly *n* groups, where each such group *g* is a restriction of *r* with the property that (a) every tuple in *g* has the same value for *X* —i.e., for all pairs of tuples *t1* and *t2* in *g*, the projections *t1*{*X*} and *t2*{*X*} are equal— and (b) no tuple of *r* not in *g* has that same value for *X*. *Note*: In fact, each such group is an equivalence class, q.v.

Example: See the example under grouping.

group (mathematics) A formal system that obeys all of The Laws of Algebra, q.v., except that (a) multiplication isn't necessarily defined and (b) addition isn't necessarily commutative (if it is, then the group is a commutative or Abelian group, otherwise it's a noncommutative group).

grouping Let r be a relation and let the heading of r be partitioned into subsets $\{X\}$ and $\{Y\}$. Let the attributes of $\{Y\}$ be $Y1, Y2, \ldots, Yn$; also, let $\{X\}$ not contain any attribute called YR. Then the grouping r GROUP ($\{Y\}$ AS YR) is another relation s. The heading of s consists of $\{X\}$ extended with an attribute YR of type RELATION $\{Y\}$. The body of s is defined as follows: First, let z be the result of r WRAP ($\{Y\}$ AS YT). Second, for each distinct X value x in z, (a) let yr be the relation whose tuples are all and only those YT values from tuples in z in which the X value is x; (b) let t be a tuple with X value x and YR value yr (and no other attributes); then, and only then, t is a tuple of s. *Note*: Given a relation r and some grouping of r, there's always an inverse ungrouping that will yield r again; however, the converse is not necessarily true. *See* ungrouping.

Example: The following expression denotes a grouping of the relation that's the current value of relvar SP:

```
SP GROUP ( { P#, QTY } AS PQ_REL )
```

That grouping is a relation *spq* of type RELATION {S# S#, PQ_REL RELATION {P# P#, QTY QTY}}. Relation *spq* contains one tuple for each distinct S# value currently appearing in relvar SP, and no other tuples. Given the sample values in Figure 1, for example, the *spq* tuple for supplier S2 has S# value S2 and PQ_REL value a relation whose body contains just the tuples <P1,300> and <P2,400>.

H

hash A specific kind of physical access path; hence, an implementation construct.

heading A set of attributes, in which (by definition) each attribute is of the form $<A,T>$, where A is an attribute name and T is the type name for attribute A. Within any given heading, (a) distinct attributes are allowed to have the same type name but not the same attribute name; (b) the number of attributes is the degree (of the heading in question). Every subset of a heading is itself a heading. *Note*: Given that it's common to refer to an attribute, informally, by its attribute name alone, it's also common to regard a heading, informally, as a set of attribute names alone.

Examples: The heading of relvar S is

```
{ <S#,S#>, <SNAME,NAME>,
          <STATUS,INTEGER>, <CITY,CHAR> }
```

The following (corresponding to a certain projection of relvar S) is also a heading:

```
{ <CITY,CHAR>, <SNAME,NAME> }
```

These two headings might be represented less formally thus:

```
{ S#, SNAME, STATUS, CITY }
```

```
{ CITY, SNAME }
```

In **Tutorial D**, they would be represented as follows:

```
{ S# S#, SNAME NAME, STATUS INTEGER, CITY CHAR }
```

```
{ CITY CHAR, SNAME NAME }
```

Heath's theorem Let A, B, and C be subsets of the heading of relvar R, such that the set theory union of A, B, and C is equal to that heading. Let AB denote the set theory union of A and B, and similarly for AC. If R satisfies the FD $A \rightarrow B$, then R is equal to the join of its projections on AB and AC. Note that the converse of this theorem is false; that is, just because R is equal to the join of its projections on AB and AC, it doesn't follow that R satisfies the FD $A \rightarrow B$. (If we replace the FD $A \rightarrow B$ by the MVD $A \rightarrow\rightarrow B$ throughout, however, the resulting statement is true in both directions; that is, R is equal to the join of its projections on AB and AC if *and only if* it satisfies the MVD $A \rightarrow\rightarrow B$. *See* multivalued dependency.)

Example: Relvar S satisfies the FD $\{S\#\} \rightarrow \{SNAME,CITY\}$, so it's equal to the join of (and can be nonloss decomposed into) its projections on $\{S\#,SNAME,CITY\}$ and $\{S\#,STATUS\}$.

horizontal decomposition Informal term for decomposition into restrictions.

host language A programming language that relies on some data sublanguage, q.v., for its database support. *Contrast* database programming language.

I

idempotence Let *Op* be a dyadic operator, and assume for definiteness that *Op* is expressed in infix style. Then *Op* is idempotent if and only if, for all x, x *Op* $x = x$.

Examples: In logic, OR and AND are both idempotent, because x OR $x = x$ and x AND $x = x$ for all x. It follows as a direct consequence that UNION and JOIN, respectively, are idempotent in relational algebra.

identity 1. (*General*) That which distinguishes a given entity from all others. 2. (*Operator*) Equality. 3. (*Logic*) Equality; also, a tautology of the form (p) EQUIV (q). 4. (*Comparison*) A Boolean expression of the form ($exp1$) = ($exp2$), where $exp1$ and $exp2$ are expressions of the same type, that's guaranteed to evaluate to TRUE regardless of the values of any variables involved. The parentheses enclosing $exp1$ and $exp2$ might not be needed in practice. 5. (*Identity value*) Let *Op* be a commutative dyadic operator, and assume for definiteness that *Op* is expressed in infix style. If there exists a value i such that i *Op* v and v *Op* i are both equal to v for all possible values v, then i is the identity, or identity value, with respect to *Op* (*see* Laws of Algebra, The). *Note*: Identity values are also known as identity elements; neutral elements; unit elements; or sometimes just as units.

Examples (fifth definition only): The dyadic operators "+", "*", OR, AND, and JOIN have identity values 0, 1, FALSE, TRUE, and TABLE_DEE, respectively. Note the last of these in particular: it means, to spell the point out, that r JOIN TABLE_DEE = TABLE_DEE JOIN $r = r$ for all possible relations r. It also means that, just as the sum of no integers is zero (*see* aggregate operator), so the join of no relations is TABLE_DEE (*see* natural join).

identity projection The projection of a given relation r on all of its attributes (i.e., $r\{H\}$, where $\{H\}$ is the heading of r). Such a projection is guaranteed to be equal to *r*. *Note*: The term is also used of a relvar; for example, the expression SP{S#,QTY,P#} denotes the identity projection of relvar SP (and its value at any given time is the identity projection of the relation that's the value of relvar SP at the time in question).

identity restriction A restriction of a given relation *r* that's equal to *r* (i.e., is equal to *r* WHERE TRUE); especially, a restriction of the form *r* WHERE *t*, where *t* is a tautology, q.v. *Note*: The term is also used of a relvar.

Examples: Given the sample values in Figure 1, the expressions S WHERE STATUS ≠ 25 and S WHERE STATUS = STATUS both denote identity restrictions (the second necessarily so, because STATUS = STATUS is a tautology).

identity value *See* identity.

IF AND ONLY IF Same as EQUIV.

IF ... THEN ... Same as IMPLIES; more precisely, IF (*p*) THEN (*q*) is defined to be the same as (*p*) IMPLIES (*q*).

IFF Same as EQUIV.

image *See* function.

image relation In **Tutorial D**, the value (a relation) denoted by an expression of the form !!*r*, where *r* is a relational expression. The symbol !! is pronounced "bang bang" or "double bang." Such an expression can appear either (a) in a WHERE clause or (b) in the ADD specification in an EXTEND invocation (in each case, wherever a relational expression can appear). For definiteness, suppose the expression !!*r2* appears in the Boolean expression *bx* in a relational expression of the form *r1* WHERE *bx* (this is a special case of case (a); case (b) and other instances of case (a) are defined analogously). Relations *r1* and *r2* here must be such that attributes with the same name are of the same type (in other words, *r1* and *r2* must be joinable); let their common attributes be *A1, A2, . . . , An* ($n \geq 0$). Then the

expression !!*r2* is semantically equivalent to the expression (*r2*)
MATCHING RELATION {TUPLE {*A1 A1, A2 A2, . . ., An An*}})
{ALL BUT *A1, A2, . . ., An*}, where, for each pair of the form *Ai Ai* ($i = 1$,
$2, . . ., n$) within the tuple selector invocation TUPLE {. . .}, the first *Ai* is
an attribute name and the second is a reference to the attribute of that name
in *r1*.

Example: The expression

```
  S WHERE ( !!SP ) { P# } = P { P# }
```

yields a relation with heading the same as that of relvar S and body
consisting of all possible tuples <*s#,sn,st,sc*> from relvar S such that
supplier *s#* supplies all parts mentioned in relvar P. (Given the sample
values of Figure 1, the result contains just the tuple for supplier S1.)
The expression overall is semantically equivalent to this one:

```
  S WHERE
  ( ( SP MATCHING RELATION
        { TUPLE { S# S# } } ) { ALL BUT S# } ) { P# } =
                                             P { P# }
```

To elaborate: Let *s* and *sp* be the current value of relvar S and the current
value of relvar SP, respectively. For a given tuple *t* in *s,* then, the
expression (actually a relation selector invocation) RELATION {TUPLE
{S# S#}} evaluates to a relation with just one attribute, S#, and just one
tuple, and that tuple contains just the S# value from *t.* So the
corresponding image relation—i.e., the one corresponding to tuple *t,*
denoted by the expression !!SP—contains just those tuples of SP that match
that tuple *t,* projected over {P#,QTY} (= {ALL BUT S#}). The projection
(!!SP){P#} thus evaluates to a relation *ps,* say, with just one attribute, P#,
giving part numbers for all parts supplied by the supplier corresponding to
tuple *t.* For that supplier, the Boolean expression (!!SP){P#} = P{P#} then
tests the corresponding relation *ps* to see if it's equal to the projection of P
on {P#}. That test will give TRUE if and only if the supplier
corresponding to tuple *t* supplies all parts mentioned in P.

Here now is an example of case (b):

```
EXTEND S { S# } ADD ( COUNT ( !!SP ) AS CT )
```

This expression yields a relation of type RELATION {S# S#, CT INTEGER}, containing one tuple for each distinct S# value currently appearing in relvar S, and no other tuples. Each such tuple contains a supplier number and a count of the number of times that supplier number currently appears in relvar SP (the expression !!SP is, again, shorthand for the expression SP MATCHING RELATION {TUPLE {S# S#}}) {ALL BUT S#}. Given the sample values in Figure 1, for example, the tuple for supplier S2 in the result has S# value S2 and CT value two, and the tuple for supplier S5 has S# value S5 and CT value zero.

immediate checking Checking an integrity constraint whenever an update is performed that might cause it to be violated. All constraint checking is immediate in the relational model. *Contrast* deferred checking.

immediate constraint An integrity constraint for which the checking is immediate (*see* immediate checking). All constraints are immediate in the relational model. *Contrast* deferred constraint.

implementation A physical realization on a real machine of the abstract machine that constitutes some given data model (in the sense of the first definition of that term). In the interest of physical data independence, the model and its implementation should be kept rigidly separate; that is, the model should have nothing whatsoever to say about any aspect of implementation.

implementation defined Term used (in the SQL standard in particular) to refer to a feature whose semantics can vary from one implementation to another but do at least have to be specified for any individual implementation. In other words, the implementation is free to decide how it will implement the feature in question, but the result of that decision must be documented. An SQL example is the maximum length of a character string.

implementation dependent Term used (in the SQL standard in particular) to refer to a feature whose semantics can vary from one implementation to another and don't even have to be specified for any individual implementation. In other words, the term effectively means "undefined"; the implementation is free to decide how it will implement the feature in question, and the result of that decision need not be documented (it might even vary from release to release). An SQL example is the full effect of an ORDER BY clause if the specifications in that clause fail to specify a total ordering.

implication If p and q are predicates, the implication (p) IMPLIES (q) is a predicate also. Let (ip) IMPLIES (iq) be an invocation of that predicate (where ip and iq are invocations of p and q, respectively). Then that invocation (ip) IMPLIES (iq) evaluates to TRUE if and only if ip evaluates to FALSE or iq evaluates to TRUE or both. (In other words, (p) IMPLIES (q) is equivalent to $(NOT(p))$ OR (q).) *Note*: In the implication (p) IMPLIES (q), p and q are the antecedent and the consequent, respectively. The parentheses enclosing them might not be needed in practice.

Examples: For people with no training in formal logic, implication is notoriously difficult to come to grips with. Consider, e.g., the proposition

```
( 2 + 2 = 4 ) IMPLIES ( the sun is a star )
```

or, in more user-friendly terms,

```
IF ( 2 + 2 = 4 ) THEN ( the sun is a star )
```

This proposition evaluates to TRUE, because the antecedent and the consequent are both true; yet whether the sun is a star clearly has nothing to do with whether $2+2 = 4$. However, the following observation might help. Of the 16 dyadic connectives (*see* connective), some but not all are given common names such as AND and OR. But those names are really nothing more than a mnemonic device—they don't have any intrinsic meaning, they're chosen simply because the connectives so named have behavior that's similar to (not necessarily the same as) that of their natural language counterparts. In particular, the connective called IMPLIES has, of the 16 connectives available, behavior that most closely resembles that of implication as usually understood in natural language. But nobody would or should claim that the two are the same thing. Moreover, the connectives are, necessarily, formally defined; that is, they're defined purely in terms of the truth values, not the meanings, of their arguments (viz., the antecedent and consequent, in the case of IMPLIES), whereas the same obviously can't be said of their natural language counterparts.

By way of another example, the proposition

```
IF ( 2 + 2 = 5 ) THEN ( Elvis lives )
```

also—perhaps even more counterintuitively—evaluates to TRUE, because the antecedent is false; yet whether Elvis is alive clearly has nothing to do with whether $2+2 = 5$. Again, part of the justification (for the fact that the implication evaluates to TRUE, that is) is just that IMPLIES is formally defined. In this case, however, there's another argument that might be a little more satisfying. Suppose the suppliers-and-parts database is subject to the constraint that red parts must be stored in London (constraint C2 from the examples under database constraint):

```
IF ( COLOR = 'Red' ) THEN ( CITY = 'London' )
```

We obviously don't want this constraint to be violated by a part that isn't red. It follows, therefore, that we want the expression overall—which is a logical implication, of course—to evaluate to TRUE if the antecedent evaluates to FALSE.

implied by FDs Given a set *s* of FDs, a given FD is implied by *s* if and only if it's a logical consequence of the FDs in *s* according to Armstrong's inference rules, q.v.

implied by superkey(s) *See* FD implied by a superkey; JD implied by superkeys; MVD implied by a superkey.

IMPLIES *See* implication.

improper inclusion Set *s1* improperly includes set *s2,* and set *s2* is improperly included in set *s1,* if and only if *s1* and *s2* are the same set.

improper subkey A subkey that's a key; in other words, a key.

improper subset Set *s2* is an improper subset of set *s1* if and only if *s2* and *s1* are the same set.

improper superkey A superkey that's a key; in other words, a key.

improper superset Set *s1* is an improper superset of set *s2* if and only if *s1* and *s2* are the same set.

inclusion *See* bag; relational inclusion; set inclusion.

inclusion dependency Let *R1* and *R2* be relvars, not necessarily distinct. Let *X1* and *X2* be a subset of the heading of *R1* and a subset of the heading of *R2,* respectively, such that there exists a possibly empty sequence of attribute renamings on *R1* that maps *X1* into *X1'* (say), where *X1'* and *X2* contain exactly the same attributes. Further, let *R2* and *R1* be subject to the constraint that, at all times, every tuple *t2* in *R2* has an *X2* value that's the *X1'* value for at least one tuple *t1* in *R1* at the time in question. Then that constraint is an inclusion dependency (IND for short), and *R2* and *R1* are the source relvar and corresponding target relvar, respectively, for that IND. *Note*: Foreign key constraints are an important special case.

Example: Suppose the suppliers-and-parts database is subject to a constraint to the effect that no part can be stored in a city unless there's at least one supplier in that city:

```
CONSTRAINT IND1 P { CITY } ⊆ S { CITY } ;
/* every part city must also */
/* be a supplier city        */
```

Note: This constraint is not satisfied by the sample values shown in Figure 1.

inclusion polymorphism By definition (*see* type inheritance), any operator that applies to values of a given type *T* necessarily applies to values of every subtype of *T*. Such an operator is thus polymorphic, and the kind of polymorphism it exhibits is called inclusion polymorphism. *Note*: An operator that applies to variables of type *T* might or might not apply to variables of some subtype of *T*. If it does, it too is said to exhibit inclusion polymorphism.

inclusive OR Term sometimes used as a synonym for OR; used primarily to distinguish it from exclusive OR, q.v.

Incoherent Principle, The See Principle of Incoherence, The.

IND Inclusion dependency.

independent projections *See* FD preservation.

index A specific kind of physical access path; hence, an implementation construct.

indirect proof *See* proof.

indirect reasoning *See modus tollens.*

indiscernibility Lack of discernibility. *See* Principle of Identity of Indiscernibles, The.

inference rule A rule for deriving a conclusion—a theorem—from a set of premises (i.e., other theorems, possibly axioms). The derivation process is known as inference. *See also* Armstrong's inference rules; constraint inference; key inference; logical system; relation type inference; tuple type inference; type inference.

information equivalence Let *s1* and *s2* be sets of relations. Then *s1* and *s2* are information equivalent if and only if every relation in *s1* is either identical to some relation in *s2* or can be derived from the relations in *s2* (*see* derived relation), and every relation in *s2* is either identical to some relation in *s1* or can be derived from the relations in *s1*.

Information Principle, The The principle that the only kind of variable allowed in a relational database is the relation variable specifically. Equivalently, a relational database contains relvars, and nothing but relvars. Yet another equivalent formulation is: at any given time, the entire information content of the database is represented in one and only one way—namely, as relations. *Note*: It has to be said that this principle isn't very well named. It might more accurately be called The Principle of Uniform Representation, or even The Principle of Uniformity of Representation, since the crucial point about it is that it implies that all information in a relational database is represented in the same way—namely, as relations.

inheritance Type inheritance, q.v.

injection A mapping, or function, from set $s1$ to set $s2$ such that each element of $s2$ is the image of at most one element of $s1$. Also known as a nonloss, injective, or "one-to-one into" mapping (though *one-to-one* here isn't being used in its strict sense, q.v.).

Example: The mapping from nonnegative integers x to their squares x^2 is an injection from the set of all nonnegative integers to itself.

inner join Same as join. The qualification *inner* is used to distinguish the join in question from its outer counterpart. Outer join in turn—at least as usually understood—has to do with nulls and three-valued logic and is therefore deliberately not discussed further in this dictionary (though in fact it would be possible to define a "respectable" form of outer join that didn't involve nulls at all).

INSERT Loosely, an operator that inserts a given set of tuples into a given relvar. It's shorthand for a certain relational assignment.

Example: The INSERT statement

```
INSERT SP
RELATION {
TUPLE { S# S#('S3'), P# P#('P1'), QTY QTY(150) },
TUPLE { S# S#('S5'), P# P#('P1'), QTY QTY(500) } } ;
```

is shorthand for the following relational assignment:

```
SP := ( SP ) UNION
       ( RELATION {
         TUPLE { S# S#('S3'), P# P#('P1'),
                                QTY QTY(150) },
         TUPLE { S# S#('S5'), P# P#('P1'),
                                QTY QTY(500) } } ) ;
```

In this example, the expressions S#('S3') and S#('S5') are selector invocations for type S#; the expression P#('P1') is a selector invocation for type P#; and the expressions QTY(150) and QTY(500) are selector invocations for type QTY. Likewise, the two expressions of the form TUPLE {...} are selector invocations for tuple type TUPLE {S# S#, P# P#, QTY QTY}, and the sole expression of the form RELATION {...} is a selector invocation for relation type RELATION {S# S#, P# P#, QTY QTY}.

Note, incidentally, that with INSERT as here defined it's not an error to try to insert a tuple that already exists in the target relvar. Replacing UNION in the expansion by D_UNION would solve this problem (if it is a problem).

instantiation Loosely, an invocation of a predicate, in which (by definition) each parameter is replaced by some argument. The result of such instantiation is a proposition. *Note*: Actually, the logical notion of instantiation is more general than the familiar programming language notion of function invocation. To be specific, we can instantiate an n-place predicate by substituting arguments for just m of its parameters ($m \leq n$), thereby obtaining an r-place predicate, where $r = n - m$. If $m = n$, the instantiation is said to be full (and the term *instantiation,* unqualified, is usually taken to mean full instantiation, unless the context demands otherwise); otherwise it's said to be partial.

integrity A database is in a state of integrity if and only if it violates no defined integrity constraints (i.e., if and only if it's consistent). Integrity is necessary but not sufficient for correctness. The relational model requires databases to be in a state of integrity at all times, where "at all times" effectively means at statement boundaries (except as noted under type constraint).

integrity constraint A named Boolean expression, or something equivalent to such an expression, that's required to be satisfied (i.e., to evaluate to TRUE) at all times, where "at all times" effectively means at statement boundaries (except as noted under type constraint). There are two basic kinds, database constraints and type constraints, q.v. (*but see* attribute constraint; relvar constraint; tuple constraint). The DBMS should reject any update that, if accepted, would cause some integrity constraint to be violated (i.e., to evaluate to FALSE). *Note*: Constraints other than type constraints constrain updates specifically, and updates by definition apply to variables specifically; thus, such constraints apply to variables specifically too—i.e., anything so constrained must be a variable, by definition.

intelligent key A single-attribute key that, in addition to its main purpose of serving to identify some entity, carries some kind of encoded information embedded within it. *Contrast* surrogate key.

Example: Let parts purchased from domestic suppliers be assigned part numbers in the range 0-4999 and parts purchased elsewhere be assigned part numbers in the range 5000-9999. Now assume the 5001st different kind of part is purchased from a domestic supplier. Clearly, the part numbering scheme will now have to be revised, and any application that previously relied on the fact that parts purchased domestically have numbers less than 5000 will now fail. As this example suggests, intelligent keys should be used with caution. (Actually, a similar remark applies to the encoding of information within *any* attribute, not just key attributes specifically, but key attributes seem to be particularly prone to this kind of abuse.)

intended interpretation For a given relvar, the informal, user-understood meaning (i.e., the relvar predicate, q.v.). Also referred to as interpretation, unqualified. *Contrast* relvar constraint (second definition).

intension For a given relation or relvar, the intended interpretation, or sometimes the heading. *Contrast* extension (third definition).

Interchangeability Principle, The (*Of base and virtual relvars*) The principle that there should be no arbitrary and unnecessary distinctions between base and virtual relvars; that is, virtual relvars should "look and feel" just like base ones so far as users are concerned.

interdependent projections *See* FD preservation.

internal predicate The total relvar constraint for a given relvar. The term is deprecated because it's at least arguably misleading (since relvar constraints are not just predicates but propositions).

interpretation Same as intended interpretation.

INTERSECT *See* intersection.

intersection 1. (*Dyadic case*) The intersection of two relations $r1$ and $r2$, $r1$ INTERSECT $r2$, where $r1$ and $r2$ are of the same type T, is a relation of type T with body the set of all tuples t such that t appears in both $r1$ and $r2$. 2. (*N-adic case*) The intersection of n relations $r1, r2, \ldots, rn$ ($n \geq 0$), INTERSECT $\{r1,r2,\ldots,rn\}$, where $r1, r2, \ldots, rn$ are all of the same type T, is a relation of type T with body the set of all tuples t such that t appears in each of $r1, r2, \ldots, rn$ (unless $n = 0$, in which case (a) some syntactic mechanism, not shown here, is needed to specify the pertinent type T and (b) the result is the universal relation, q.v., of that type). *Note*: The relational intersection operator differs in certain respects from the mathematical or set theory operator of the same name, q.v. In fact, it's a special case of join, q.v.

Example: The expression (S{CITY}) INTERSECT (P{CITY}) denotes the intersection of the projections on {CITY} of the relations that are the current values of relvars S and P. That intersection is a relation of type RELATION {CITY CHAR}. Moreover, if the current values of relvars S and P are *s* and *p,* respectively, the body of that relation consists of all tuples of the form <*c*> that appear in both *s*{CITY} and *p*{CITY}— meaning *c* is a current supplier city that's also a current part city. Note that the expression (S{CITY}) INTERSECT (P{CITY}) is semantically equivalent to the expression (S{CITY}) JOIN (P{CITY}).

intersection (bag theory) *See* bag.

intersection (set theory) The set of all elements appearing in both of two given sets. *Note*: This definition can obviously be extended to apply to any number of sets.

intersection star *See* bag.

into (*Of a function*; *used as an adjective*) Having range equal to some proper subset of the codomain (*contrast* onto). *See* injection.

inverse *See* Laws of Algebra, The.

Examples: 1. In ordinary arithmetic, the identities for "+" and "*" are 0 and 1, respectively (*see* identity). As a consequence, (a) for "+", the inverse of x is $-x$; (b) for "*", the inverse of x is $1/x$ (unless x is 0, the only number that has no multiplicative inverse). 2. In two-valued logic, the identities for OR and AND are FALSE and TRUE, respectively (again, *see* identity). As a consequence, (a) for OR, FALSE is its own inverse but TRUE has no inverse (there's no truth value v such that TRUE OR v yields FALSE); (b) for AND, TRUE is its own inverse but FALSE has no inverse (there's no truth value v such that FALSE AND v yields TRUE).

involution 1. (*Logic*) If *v* is a truth value, then the negation of the negation of *v* is equal to *v*. 2. (*Set theory*) If *s* is a set, then the complement of the complement of *s* is equal to *s*.

irreducibility 1. (*Of a key*) *See* candidate key. 2. (*Of a relvar*) Sixth normal form. 3. (*Of an FD*) Left irreducible. 4. (*Of a set of FDs*) The set *s* of FDs is irreducible if and only if (a) the dependant in every FD in *s* contains just one attribute, (b) every FD in *s* is left irreducible, and (c) no FD can be removed from *s* without changing the closure of *s*.

irreducibly dependent (*Of a dependant in an FD*) Let *A* and *B* be subsets of the heading of some relvar *R*. Then *B* is irreducibly dependent on *A* if and only if it's functionally dependent on *A* and not on any proper subset of *A*.

Examples: In relvar S, {STATUS} is irreducibly dependent on {S#}; it's also dependent on {S#,CITY}, but not irreducibly so. Similarly, in relvar SP, {QTY} is irreducibly dependent on {S#,P#}; it's also dependent on {S#,P#,QTY}, but not irreducibly so.

irreducibly equivalent (*Of a set of FDs*) Let *s1* and *s2* be sets of FDs. Then *s1* is irreducibly equivalent to *s2* if and only if it's equivalent to *s2* and irreducible.

IS_EMPTY A **Tutorial D** operator that returns TRUE or FALSE according to whether a specified relation is empty or not.

isomorphism Let *sX* and *sY* be sets, not necessarily distinct, and let *f* be a bijective mapping from *sX* to *sY*. Let *OpX* be an operator that takes elements of *sX* as its operands and yields an element of *sX* as its result. Then *f* is an isomorphism if and only if, for all such operators *OpX*, there exists an analogous operator *OpY* that takes elements of *sY* as its operands and yields an element of *sY* as its result such that, whenever *OpX* applied to *x1, x2, . . ., xn* yields *x*, then *OpY* applied to *y1, y2, . . ., yn* yields *y*, where *y1, y2, . . ., yn*, and *y* are the images of *x1, x2, . . ., xn*, and *x*, respectively, under *f*. In other words, a bijective mapping is an isomorphism if and only if it preserves the algebraic structure of the domain sX in the codomain sY. *Note*: If the bijective mapping f is an isomorphism, then its inverse is an isomorphism as well.

Example: Let sX be the set {EVEN,ODD} and let operators "+" and "$*$" be defined as follows:

+	EVEN	ODD
EVEN	EVEN	ODD
ODD	ODD	EVEN

$*$	EVEN	ODD
EVEN	EVEN	EVEN
ODD	EVEN	ODD

Now let sY be the set {TRUE, FALSE} and let f be a bijection from sX to sY that maps EVEN and ODD to TRUE and FALSE, respectively. Further, let the logical operators EQUIV and OR correspond to "+" and "$*$", respectively. Then f is an isomorphism from sX (with its operators "+" and "$*$") to sY (with its operators EQUIV and OR).

J

JD Join dependency.

JD implied by superkeys The JD ✿{*A1,A2,. . .,An*} is implied by superkeys if and only if (a) each of *A1, A2, . . ., An* is a superkey for the pertinent relvar *R* and (b) the keys of *R* can be ordered in such a way that for each such key, at least one of *A1, A2,. . ., An* includes both that key and its successor with respect to that ordering.

Example: Let relvar R have attributes A, B, C, D, E, and F (only), and let it have keys {A}, {B}, and {C} (only). Let ABD denote the set of attributes {A,B,D}, and similarly for other letter combinations. Then the first of the following JDs is implied by the superkeys of R but the second and third aren't:

```
✿ { ABD, BCE, CF }
✿ { ABD, CE,  CF }
✿ { ABD, BCE, DF }
```

Note that relvar R necessarily satisfies the first of these JDs and fails to satisfy the second (it might not be obvious that this latter claim is valid, but in fact it is). The third JD might or might not be satisfied. If it is, relvar R isn't in 5NF; conversely, if relvar R is in 5NF, it can't possibly satisfy the third JD.

JOIN *See* natural join.

join Natural join, q.v. (unless the context demands otherwise).

joinable 1. (*Dyadic case*) Relations *r1* and *r2* are joinable if and only if attributes with the same name are of the same type—equivalently, if and only if the set theory union of their headings is a legal heading.
2. (*N-adic case*) Relations *r1, r2, . . . , rn* (*n* > 0) are joinable if and only if for all *i, j* relations *ri* and *rj* are joinable ($1 \leq i \leq n,\ 1 \leq j \leq n$).

join dependency A generalization of the concept of multivalued dependency (every multivalued dependency is a join dependency, but some join dependencies aren't multivalued dependencies). A join dependency is an expression—actually a proposition—of the form ✪{*A1,A2,...,An*}, where *A1, A2, ..., An* are all subsets of the heading of the same relvar *R*, and the expression overall is read as "star *A1, A2, ..., An*." Relvar *R* satisfies the join dependency (JD) ✪{*A1,A2,...,An*}—equivalently, that JD holds in relvar *R*—if and only if every relation that's a legal value for *R* is equal to the join of its projections on *A1, A2, ..., An. Note*: Join dependency is also known as join dependence. Observe that relvar *R* can't possibly satisfy the JD ✪{*A1,A2,...,An*} unless the set theory union of *A1, A2, ..., An* is equal to the heading of *R*. Observe further that it's immediate from the definition that relvar *R* can be nonloss decomposed into its projections on *A1, A2, ..., An* if and only if it satisfies the JD ✪{*A1,A2,...,An*}. Note finally that from a formal point of view, a JD ✪{*A1,A2,...,An*} is just a proposition that, by definition, can be either satisfied or not (i.e., can evaluate to either TRUE or FALSE); informally, however, it's common to define ✪{*A1,A2,...,An*} to be a JD only if it's actually satisfied by the pertinent relvar. But that definition leaves no way of saying that a given relvar fails to satisfy, or violates, some JD (because, by that definition, a JD that isn't satisfied isn't a JD!).

Example: Relvar S satisfies the JD

```
✪ { { S#, SNAME }, { S#, STATUS }, { S#, CITY } }
```

because every relation that's a legal value for S is equal to the join of its projections on {S#,SNAME}, {S#,STATUS}, and {S#,CITY}; i.e., relvar S could be nonloss decomposed into those three projections. (Of course, there's no requirement that this decomposition actually be performed— whether it should or not depends on whether there's any advantage to be gained by doing so.)

join trap *See* connection trap.

K

key A candidate key, q.v. (unless the context demands otherwise).

key attribute An attribute of a given relvar that's part of at least one key of that relvar. *See also* subkey.

key constraint A constraint to the effect that a given subset of the heading of a given relvar is a key for that relvar. In **Tutorial D**, such a constraint is defined by means of a KEY specification within the pertinent relvar definition (*see*, e.g., the definitions for relvars S, P, and SP in the introduction to this dictionary). Note, however, that while the system will certainly enforce the uniqueness property implied by such a constraint—*see* candidate key—it can't in general enforce the corresponding irreducibility property as well. In other words, specifying KEY$\{K\}$ as part of the definition of relvar R means that K is certainly a superkey, q.v., but not necessarily a key as such, for relvar R.

Example: Suppose we were to specify KEY$\{$S#,CITY$\}$ instead of KEY$\{$S#$\}$ in the definition of relvar S. Then the system obviously won't be able to enforce the constraint that supplier numbers as such, as opposed to supplier-number/city combinations, are unique. (On the other hand, if we were to specify both $\{$S#$\}$ and $\{$S#,CITY$\}$ as keys, the system should at least be able to recognize that the former is a proper subset of the latter and so reject the latter specification.)

key inference The process of determining the key constaints that apply to a given derived relvar or are satisfied by a given derived relation. Key inference is a special case of constraint inference, q.v.

L

Laws of Algebra, The Let A be an algebra, q.v., consisting of a set s of elements $x, y, z, \ldots$ together with two distinct dyadic operators "+" and "∗" (usually called addition and multiplication, respectively, though they aren't necessarily the operators known by those names in conventional arithmetic). Then The Laws of Algebra are as follows:

- *Closure laws*: The set s is closed under both "+" and "∗"; that is, for all x and y in s, each of the expressions $x+y$ and $x∗y$ yields an element of s.

- *Commutative laws*: For all x and y in s, $x+y = y+x$ and $x∗y = y∗x$.

- *Associative laws*: For all $x, y,$ and z in s, $x+(y+z) = (x+y)+z$ and $x∗(y∗z) = (x∗y)∗z$.

- *Identity laws*: There exist elements 0 and 1 in s such that for all x in s, $x+0 = x$ and $x∗1 = x$. The elements 0 and 1 are called the additive identity and the multiplicative identity, respectively.

- *Inverse laws*: For all x in s, there exist elements $-x$ and (unless $x = 0$) $1/x$ in s such that $x+(-x) = 0$ and $x∗(1/x) = 1$. The elements $-x$ and $1/x$ are called the additive inverse and the multiplicative inverse, respectively (of x in each case). The expressions $x+(-y)$ and $x∗(1/y)$ are usually abbreviated to $x-y$ and x/y, respectively.

- *Distributive law* (of "∗" over "+"): For all $x, y,$ and z in s, $x∗(y+z) = (x∗y)+(x∗z)$.

Note, however, that not all algebras abide by all of the foregoing laws. In the algebra of sets, for example, the "+" and "∗" operators are union and intersection, respectively, but the inverse laws don't hold for these operations.

left irreducible FD Given a set s of FDs, the FD f in s is left irreducible (with respect to s) if and only if no attribute can be removed from the determinant of f without changing the closure of s.

Examples: Let s be the set of all FDs satisfied by relvar SP. Then the FDs {S#,P#} → {QTY} and {S#,P#,QTY} → {QTY} both appear in s. Of these two FDs, the first is left irreducible but the second isn't.

left associativity Let Op be a dyadic operator, and assume for definiteness that Op is expressed in infix style. Then Op is left associative if and only if, for all x, y, and z, $x\ Op\ y\ Op\ z = (x\ Op\ y)\ Op\ z$; similarly, it's right associative if and only if, for all x, y, and z, $x\ Op\ y\ Op\ z = x\ Op\ (y\ Op\ z)$. *Note*: In mathematics and logic, left and right associativity both reduce to associativity as normally understood (q.v.). However, such is not necessarily the case in computing. For example, consider what happens if x, y, and z are numbers and Op is "+". In this case, the expressions $(x+y)+z$ and $x+(y+z)$ might well produce different results; it might even be that one causes an overflow and the other doesn't.

less-than join A theta join in which theta is "<".

lexical Pertaining to individual words and other basic symbols (punctuation, etc.) of a language. *Contrast* semantic; syntactic.

literal 1. (*Programming languages*) Loosely, a self-defining symbol; a symbol that denotes a value that can be determined at compile time. More precisely, a literal is a symbol that denotes a value that's fixed and determined by the symbol in question (and the type of that value is therefore also fixed and determined by the symbol in question). Every value of every type, tuple and relation types included, must be denotable by means of some literal. Note that a literal is a special case of a selector invocation (*see* selector). Note too that there's a logical difference between a literal as such and the value it denotes (*see* constant). 2. (*Logic*) A simple proposition or its negation; a simple predicate or its negation (*see* simple predicate; simple proposition).

Examples (*first definition only*): 4 (a literal of type INTEGER); 'ABC' (a literal of type CHAR); FALSE (a literal of type BOOLEAN); S#('S1') (a literal of type S#); TUPLE {S# S#('S1'), P# P#('P1'), QTY QTY(300)} (a literal of type TUPLE {S# S#, P# P#, QTY QTY}); RELATION {TUPLE {S# S#('S1'), P# P#('P1'), QTY QTY(300)}} (a literal of type RELATION {S# S#, P# P#, QTY QTY}); and so on.

logic The science or scientific study of the methods and principles used in valid reasoning.

logic variable A variable that can appear either bound or free in predicate calculus expressions (*see* bound variable; free variable); not to be confused with a logical variable, q.v. *See also* range variable.

logical data independence *See* data independence.

logical database design The process (or the result of the process) of deciding, given some body of data to be represented in some database, what relvars that database should contain, what attributes they should have, and what constraints they should be subject to. Ideally, the goal is to produce a design that's independent of all considerations having to with either physical implementation or specific applications—the latter objective being desirable for the good reason that it's generally not the case that all uses to which the database will be put are known at design time. Overall, the design process can be summarized as one of (a) pinning down the relvar predicates (as well as other "business rules," possibly) as carefully as possible, albeit necessarily somewhat informally, and then (b) mapping those predicates and rules to specific relvars and formal constraints.

logical equivalence *See* equivalence.

logical expression An expression denoting a truth value.

logical implication Implication, q.v.

logical operator An operator that (a) takes either values or variables (or both) of type BOOLEAN as operands and (b) either returns a value, or updates at least one variable, of type BOOLEAN. The connectives are a special case.

logical system Loosely, a system consisting of axioms and inference rules, together with a set of theorems that can be derived from the former by means of the latter. More precisely, a logical system consists of (a) a set of symbols (e.g., NOT, AND, punctuation symbols, variable names); (b) a set of grammatical rules for forming "sentences" of the system; (c) a set of given sentences (the axioms); and (d) a set of rules for inferring "new" sentences from "old" ones (the rules of inference).

Examples: Propositional logic and predicate logic are both logical systems, in which the legal sentences are propositions and predicates, respectively.

logical variable (*Programming languages*) A variable of type BOOLEAN. The term is best avoided because of possible confusion with the term *logic variable,* q.v.

lossless decomposition Nonloss decomposition, q.v.

lossy decomposition A decomposition that isn't nonloss.

Example: The decomposition of relvar S into its projections on {S#,SNAME} and {SNAME,STATUS,CITY} is lossy because it isn't guaranteed that, at all times, S is equal to the join of those projections.

M

managed redundancy Controlled redundancy, q.v.

mandatory participation *See* cardinality constraint.

many-to-many correspondence Strictly, a rule pairing two sets *s1* and *s2* (*s1* and *s2* not necessarily distinct) such that each element of *s1* corresponds to at least one element of *s2* and each element of *s2* corresponds to at least one element of *s1*; equivalently, that pairing itself. Often used loosely, however, to mean a pairing such that either (a) each element of *s1* corresponds to any number of elements of *s2* (possibly none at all) and each element of *s2* corresponds to at least one element of *s1,* or (b) each element of *s1* corresponds to at least one element of *s2* and each element of *s2* corresponds to any number of elements of *s1* (possibly none at all), or (c) each element of *s1* corresponds to any number of elements of *s2* (possibly none at all) and each element of *s2* corresponds to any number of elements of *s1* (possibly none at all). The term is best avoided unless the intended meaning is clear.

Example (*strict sense only*): Let *s* be the set of all positive integers. Consider the pairing of positive integers *x* and *y* defined as follows: Positive integers *x* and *y* are paired if and only if they have the same number of digits in conventional decimal notation (no leading zeros). Then that pairing is a many-to-many correspondence from *s* to itself.

many-to-one correspondence Strictly, a rule pairing two sets *s1* and *s2* (*s1* and *s2* not necessarily distinct) such that each element of *s1* corresponds to exactly one element of *s2* and each element of *s2* corresponds to at least one element of *s1* (in other words, a surjection, q.v.); equivalently, that pairing itself. Often used loosely, however, to mean a pairing such that (a) each element of *s1* corresponds to at most one element of *s2* and each element of *s2* corresponds to at least one element of *s1,* or (b) each element of *s1* corresponds to exactly one element of *s2* and each element of *s2* corresponds to any number of elements of *s1* (possibly none at all), or (c) each element of *s1* corresponds to at most one element of *s2* and each element of *s2* corresponds to any number of elements of *s1* (possibly none at all). The term is best avoided unless the intended meaning is clear.

Example (*strict sense only*): Let *s1* and *s2* be the set of all integers and the set of all nonnegative integers, respectively. Then the pairing of integers x with their absolute values $|x|$ is a many-to-one correspondence from *s1* to *s2*.

many-valued logic Same as nVL, q.v., for some $n > 2$.

map / mapping A function, q.v. Also used (in this dictionary in particular, on occasion) to mean a function that's a bijection specifically, together with its inverse.

mark *See* null.

MATCHING *See* semijoin.

material equivalence Logical equivalence, q.v.

material implication Logical implication, q.v.

materialization 1. An implementation technique in which an intermediate result relation is produced in its entirety before being passed on to another operation. *Contrast* pipelining. 2. View materialization, q.v.

materialized view Deprecated term for a snapshot. Note the difference between (a) materialization as a technique for implementing operations on views (*see* view materialization) and (b) a "materialized view"—i.e., a snapshot—as such. The former is an implementation technique and should have no logical consequences for the user at all (i.e., users shouldn't need to know whether a given operation on a given view is implemented by materialization). By contrast, the latter is an issue that concerns the user very much; that is, the user certainly does need to know whether a given relvar is a snapshot, because whether it is or not affects the semantics of the relvar in question. The problem is, however, that (as the definition indicates) snapshots have come to be known, at least in some circles, not as snapshots at all but as materialized views. But snapshots aren't views; views are virtual and snapshots aren't, and "materialized view" is a contradiction in terms (at least as far as the model is concerned). Worse yet, the unqualified term *view* is often taken nowadays to mean a materialized view specifically, and we're thus in danger of no longer having a good term for a view in the original sense. This dictionary does use *view* in its original sense, but be warned that the term doesn't always have that meaning elsewhere. *Caveat lector.*

meaning (*Of a relvar*) *See* intended interpretation; relvar constraint (second definition); relvar predicate.

member An element of a bag or set.

membership *See* bag membership; set membership.

merge A join implementation technique.

metadata Data about data. *See* catalog.

minimality (*Of a key or set of FDs*) Old fashioned and somewhat deprecated (because inaccurate) term for irreducibility.

MINUS *See* difference.

missing information A term often used to refer to information that's either currently unknown or not applicable. *Note*: To say that information that's currently unknown is missing is possibly reasonable. However, to say that information that's not applicable is missing isn't reasonable at all (and the usage is therefore deprecated). For example, if a given employee is unmarried, spouse information for that employee isn't missing—rather, it simply doesn't exist.

model Either a data model in general (usually in the sense of the first definition of that term) or the relational model specifically, as the context demands. *Note*: Actually, the term *model* has been given a great number of other meanings as well in the literature—more meanings, in fact, than it can reasonably be expected to bear. Such additional meanings are deliberately omitted here.

modus ponens Loosely, "proof by affirmation"; a rule of inference to the effect that if we know that (p) IMPLIES (q) and p are both true, we can infer that q is true. Also known as direct reasoning.

modus tollens Loosely, "proof by denial"; a rule of inference to the effect that if we know that (p) IMPLIES (q) is true and q is false, we can infer that p is false. Also known as indirect reasoning.

monadic (*Of an operator*) Having exactly one operand; that is, being defined in terms of exactly one parameter.

multi-relvar constraint Term sometimes used for a database constraint that mentions two or more distinct relvars. *Contrast* single-relvar constraint. *Note*: The difference between single-relvar and multi-relvar constraints is more a matter of pragma than logic, thanks to The Principle of Interchangeability among other things.

Examples: The foreign key constraints from relvar SP to relvars S and P; also constraint C3 from the examples under database constraint.

multi-tuple constraint Term sometimes used for a relvar or database constraint that isn't a single-tuple constraint, q.v.

Example: Constraint C3 from the examples under database constraint might be regarded as a multi-tuple constraint.

multidependent *See* multivalued dependency.

multidetermines *See* multivalued dependency.

multiple assignment An operation that allows several individual assignments all to be performed "simultaneously," without any integrity checking being done until all of the individual assignments have been executed in their entirety. Note that multiple assignments are involved implicitly in a variety of other operations—for example, updating some join view, or updating some relvar in such a way as to cause some compensating action (q.v.) to be performed.

Example: The following "double DELETE" is, logically, a multiple assignment operation:

```
DELETE S  WHERE S# = S#('S1') ,
DELETE SP WHERE S# = S#('S1') ;
```

Note the comma separator after the first DELETE, which indicates syntactically that the end of the overall statement hasn't yet been reached. Note too that the semantics would remain completely unchanged if the two individual DELETEs were specified in reverse order. Here's the expanded form:

```
S  := S  WHERE NOT ( S# = S#('S1') ) ,
SP := SP WHERE NOT ( S# = S#('S1') ) ;
```

multiplicity *See* bag.

multiset Same as bag.

multivalued dependency A generalization of the concept of functional dependency (every functional dependency is a multivalued dependency, but some multivalued dependencies aren't functional dependencies). A multivalued dependency is an expression—actually a proposition—of the form $A \twoheadrightarrow B$, where A and B are both subsets of the heading of the same relvar R, and the expression overall is read as "B is multidependent on A," or "A multidetermines B," or, more simply, just "A double arrow B." Let C be a subset of the heading of that same relvar R such that the set theory union of A, B, and C is equal to that heading. Let AB denote the set theory union of A and B, and similarly for AC. Then relvar R satisfies the multivalued dependencies (MVDs) $A \twoheadrightarrow B$ and $A \twoheadrightarrow C$—equivalently, those MVDs hold in relvar R—if and only if R satisfies the join dependency ☼{AB,AC}. *Note*: Multivalued dependency is also known as multivalued dependence. Observe that A and B in the MVD $A \rightarrow\rightarrow B$ are, specifically, sets of attributes. Informally, however, it's common (though strictly incorrect) to speak of the attributes in B as if those attributes per se, instead of the set B that contains those attributes, were multidependent on A. Likewise, it's common (though strictly incorrect) to speak of the attributes in A as if B were multidependent on those attributes per se, instead of on the set A that contains those attributes. Note that it follows from the definition that if relvar R satisfies the MVDs $A \rightarrow\rightarrow B$ and $A \rightarrow\rightarrow C$, then if it contains the tuples $<a,b1,c1>$ and $<a,b2,c2>$, it also contains the tuples $<a,b1,c2>$ and $<a,b2,c1>$. Note further that it's also immediate from the definition that relvar R can be nonloss decomposed into its projections on AB and AC if and only if it satisfies the MVDs $A \rightarrow\rightarrow B$ and $A \rightarrow\rightarrow C$ (this theorem, a stronger form of Heath's theorem, is one of many due to Fagin). Note finally that from a formal point of view, an MVD $A \rightarrow\rightarrow B$ is just a proposition that, by definition, can be either satisfied or not (i.e., can evaluate to either TRUE or FALSE); informally, however, it's common to define $A \rightarrow\rightarrow B$ to be an MVD only if it's actually satisfied by the pertinent relvar. But that definition leaves no way of saying that a given relvar fails to satisfy, or violates, some MVD (because, by that definition, an MVD that isn't satisfied isn't an MVD!).

mutation Term sometimes used (especially in OO contexts) for updating.

mutator Term sometimes used (especially in OO contexts) for an update operator. (SQL's use of the term is unorthodox, in that its mutators are read-only.)

MVD Multivalued dependency.

MVD implied by a superkey The MVD $A \rightarrow\rightarrow B$ is implied by a superkey if and only if A is a superkey for the pertinent relvar.

N

***n*-adic** (*Of an operator*) Having exactly *n* operands; i.e., being defined in terms of exactly *n* parameters ($n \geq 0$). *Note:* Let *Op* be a dyadic operator. If we want to define an *n*-adic version of *Op*, then it's necessary—at least if that *n*-adic version is intended to apply to a set, as opposed to a sequence, of operands—that *Op* be both commutative and associative. Examples of such operators defined in this dictionary include (a) the logical operators AND, EQUIV, OR, and XOR and (b) the relational operators intersect, join, product, and union.

***n*-ary** (Of a heading, key, tuple, tuplevar, relation, or relvar) Of degree n ($n \geq 0$).

***n*-place** (*Of a predicate*) Same as *n*-adic ($n \geq 0$).

***n*-tuple** A tuple of degree *n* ($n \geq 0$).

NAND In logic, a dyadic connective (also known as the Sheffer stroke and usually written as a vertical bar, "|"); if *p* and *q* are predicates, then $(p)|(q)$ is a predicate also. Let $(ip)|(iq)$ be an invocation of that predicate (where *ip* and *iq* are invocations of *p* and *q*, respectively). Then that invocation $(ip)|(iq)$ evaluates to FALSE if and only if *ip* and *iq* both evaluate to TRUE. (In other words, $(p)|(q)$ is equivalent to NOT$((p)$ AND $(q))$.) *Note:* The parentheses enclosing *p* and *q* in the expression $(p)|(q)$ might not be needed in practice. Also, NAND as just defined is a logical operator; however, the algebra **A**, q.v., includes an operator called NAND that—by definition—is an algebraic operator instead (it's basically "complement of join").

natural join 1. (*Dyadic case*) Let relations *r1* and *r2* be such that attributes with the same name are of the same type (in other words, let *r1* and *r2* be joinable, q.v.). Then the natural join of *r1* and *r2*, *r1* JOIN *r2*, is a relation with heading the set theory union of the headings of *r1* and *r2* and with body the set of all tuples *t* such that *t* is the set theory union of a tuple from *r1* and a tuple from *r2*. 2. (*N-adic case*) Let relations *r1, r2, . . ., rn* (*n* ≥ 0) be such that attributes with the same name are of the same type (in other words, let *r1, r2, . . ., rn* be joinable, q.v.). Then the natural join JOIN {*r1,r2,. . .,rn*} is defined as follows: If *n* = 0, the result is TABLE_DEE; if *n* = 1, the result is *r1*; otherwise, choose any two distinct relations from the set *r1, r2, . . ., rn* and replace them by their (dyadic) natural join, and repeat this process until the set consists of just one relation *r*, which is the overall result.

Example: The expression S JOIN SP denotes the natural join of the relations that are the current values of relvars S and SP. That join is a relation of type RELATION {S# S#, SNAME NAME, STATUS INTEGER, CITY CHAR, P# P#, QTY QTY}. Moreover, if the current values of relvars S and SP are *s* and *sp*, respectively, the body of that relation consists of all tuples of the form <*s#,sn,st,sc,p#,q*> such that the tuple <*s#,sn,st,sc*> appears in *s* and the tuple <*s#,p#,q*> appears in *sp*.

negation If *p* is a predicate, its negation NOT(*p*) is a predicate also. Let NOT(*ip*) be an invocation of that predicate (where *ip* is an invocation of *p*). Then that invocation NOT(*ip*) evaluates to TRUE if and only if *ip* evaluates to FALSE. *Note*: The parentheses enclosing *p* in the expression NOT(*p*) might not be needed in practice.

negation as failure A concept closely related to The Closed World Assumption, q.v.; it means, loosely, that if a given tuple could appear in the result of a given query (at least in principle) but doesn't, then the proposition represented by that tuple is false.

negative Strictly less than zero. (The expression -0 is legal, of course, but it doesn't denote a negative value; rather, it denotes the nonnegative value 0.)

nested relation *See* relation valued attribute.

NF² NF squared; short for NFNF ("non first normal form"). An NF² relvar is, loosely, a relvar with at least one relation valued attribute. The term is deprecated, however, because it's based on a flawed understanding of the concept of first normal form. Also, the NF² concept is usually taken to include certain extensions to the conventional relational operators, extensions that aren't just shorthand and thus aren't included (or needed) in the relational model.

niladic (*Of an operator*) Having no operands; i.e., being defined in terms of no parameters. *Note*: An operator might appear to be niladic syntactically and yet not be limited to having the same effect on every invocation, owing to its use of what might be called hidden operands such as the system clock. Indeed, such "niladic" operators—which are, of course, not truly niladic anyway—are the normal case.

Example: Many languages provide an operator for generating random (or, rather, "pseudorandom") numbers. Such operators effectively have a hidden operand: namely, the random number returned on the previous invocation.

noncommutative group *See* group (mathematics).

nonkey attribute An attribute of a given relvar that isn't part of any key of that relvar.

nonloss decomposition Replacing a relvar R by its projections $R1$, $R2, \ldots, Rn$, such that (a) the join of $R1, R2, \ldots, Rn$ is guaranteed to be equal to R, and usually also such that (b) each of $R1, R2, \ldots, Rn$ is needed in order to provide that guarantee (i.e., none of those projections is redundant in the join). Note that one "nonloss decomposition" that's always available for any given relvar R is to "replace" R by the corresponding identity projection, q.v.

Example: A nonloss decomposition that might be applied to the suppliers-and-parts database would be to replace relvar S by its projections on {S#,SNAME} and {S#,STATUS,CITY}. Relvar S could then be reconstructed by joining those two projections back together again.

nonnegative Greater than or equal to zero. *Contrast* positive.

nonscalar Not scalar. The most important nonscalar constructs in the relational model are tuples and (especially) relations themselves.

nontrivial (*Of an FD, JD, or MVD*) Not trivial. *See* trivial FD; trivial JD; trivial MVD.

NOR In logic, a dyadic connective (also known as the Peirce arrow and usually written as a down arrow, "$\downarrow$"); if p and q are predicates, then $(p)\downarrow(q)$ is a predicate also. Let $(ip)\downarrow(iq)$ be an invocation of that predicate (where ip and iq are invocations of p and q, respectively). Then that invocation $(ip)\downarrow(iq)$ evaluates to TRUE if and only if ip and iq both evaluate to FALSE. (In other words, $(p)\downarrow(q)$ is equivalent to NOT$((p)$ OR $(q))$.) *Note*: The parentheses enclosing p and q in the expression $(p)\downarrow(q)$ might not be needed in practice. Also, NOR as just defined is a logical operator; however, the algebra **A**, q.v., includes an operator called NOR that—by definition—is an algebraic operator instead (it's basically "complement of union," though "union" here refers not to the relational operator of that name but to a generalized form of that operator).

normal form 1. (*General*) Canonical form. 2. (*Of a relvar*) *See* first normal form; second normal form; and so on. *Note*: The most important relational normal forms are BCNF and 5NF (and 6NF); the others are of mainly historical interest.

normalization Using the principles of nonloss decomposition to replace some given relvar by certain of its projections, such that the join of those projections is guaranteed to be equal to the original relvar. Observe, therefore, that projection is the decomposition operator, and join the recomposition operator, with respect to the normalization process (as this latter term is usually understood). The objective of normalization is to reduce redundancy, q.v., and thereby to eliminate certain update anomalies, q.v., that might otherwise occur.

normalization principles A relvar not in 5NF should be decomposed into a set of 5NF projections; the original relvar should be reconstructable by joining those projections back together again; the decomposition process should preserve dependencies; every projection should be needed in the reconstruction process.

normalized That property of relations, and hence of relvars, according to which every tuple in the relation or relvar in question contains exactly one value (of the appropriate type) for each of its attributes. Actually, a "tuple" that didn't contain exactly one value of the appropriate type for each of its attributes wouldn't be a tuple in the first place; likewise, a "relation" that contained such a "tuple" wouldn't be a relation, and a "relvar" whose value was such a "relation" wouldn't be a relvar, either. In other words, it's immediate from the definition that all relations, and hence all relvars, are normalized. *Note*: Relvars in particular are equivalently said to be in first normal form, 1NF, q.v.; that is, a normalized relvar is just a relvar that's in 1NF, which is to say it's just a relvar. However, the term *normalized* is frequently, though inaccurately, used to refer to some normal form higher than just first (especially either BCNF or 5NF).

normalized relvar A relvar. (Relvars are always normalized by definition, in the sense that they're in at least first normal form.)

NOT *See* negation. *Note*: NOT as conventionally understood is a logical operator; however, the algebra **A**, q.v., includes an operator called NOT that—by definition—is an algebraic operator instead (it's basically "complement").

NOT MATCHING *See* semidifference.

null A construct, used in SQL in particular, for representing missing information, q.v. *Note:* By definition, nulls aren't values (they're sometimes said to be *marks*); it follows that a "type" that "contains a null" isn't a type, a "tuple" that "contains a null" isn't a tuple, a "relation" that "contains a null" isn't a relation, and a "relvar" that contains a null isn't a relvar. It follows further that nulls do serious violence to the relational model, and this dictionary therefore has very little to say regarding most null-related concepts.

null set Deprecated term sometimes used (most unfortunately!) to mean the empty set.

nullary Of degree zero. The term is probably best avoided because of the potential confusion with null, q.v.

nullary foreign key A foreign key of degree zero.

nullary heading The empty heading; that is, the heading of degree zero.

nullary key An empty key; that is, a key of degree zero.

nullary projection 1. (*Of a relation*) The projection of a given relation r on no attributes (i.e., $r\{\}$); the result is TABLE_DUM if r is empty and TABLE_DEE otherwise. 2. (*Of a tuple*) The projection of a given tuple on no attributes; the result is always the empty tuple.

nullary relation A relation of degree zero. There are exactly two such, TABLE_DEE and TABLE_DUM.

nullary tuple The empty tuple; i.e., the tuple of degree zero.

nullology The study of the empty set. The term has nothing to do with null, q.v.

***n*VL** A logic with n "truth values"; in other words, n-valued logic for some $n \geq 2$. *Note:* If $n = 2$, those "truth values" really are truth values, and we can drop the quotation marks.

O

object A thing.

object class *See* class (second definition).

object ID A pointer, q.v.

object modeling *See* semantic modeling.

object oriented / object orientation Leaning toward things.

object/relational database A relational database (*see* object/relational DBMS).

object/relational DBMS A relational DBMS. *Note*: In practice, the major distinction between commercial DBMSs that provide "object/relational" support and those that don't is simply that the former allow users to define their own types. But a true relational DBMS does so too, and a DBMS that doesn't provide such support thus can't reasonably claim to be fully relational, even if it supports other aspects of the relational model. The fact is, the term *object/relational* is little more than a marketing label, dreamt up to conceal the fact that early "relational" products weren't very relational at all. Hence the present definition, to the effect that "object/relational" just means relational.

observer Term sometimes used (especially in OO contexts) for a read-only operator.

one-to-many correspondence Strictly, a rule pairing two sets $s1$ and $s2$ ($s1$ and $s2$ not necessarily distinct) such that each element of $s1$ corresponds to at least one element of $s2$ and each element of $s2$ corresponds to exactly one element of $s1$; equivalently, that pairing itself. Often used loosely, however, to mean a pairing such that either (a) each element of $s1$ corresponds to any number of elements of $s2$ (possibly none at all) and each element of $s2$ corresponds to exactly one element of $s1$, or

(b) each element of *s1* corresponds to at least one element of *s2* and each element of *s2* corresponds to at most one element of *s1,* or (c) each element of *s1* corresponds to any number of elements of *s2* (possibly none at all) and each element of *s2* corresponds to at most one element of *s1.* The term is best avoided unless the intended meaning is clear.

Example (*strict sense only*): Let *s1* and *s2* be the set of all nonnegative numbers and the set of all numbers, respectively. Then the pairing of nonnegative numbers *x* with their square roots $\pm\sqrt{x}$ is a one-to-many correspondence from *s1* to *s2.*

one-to-one correspondence Strictly, a rule pairing two sets *s1* and *s2* (*s1* and *s2* not necessarily distinct) such that each element of *s1* corresponds to exactly one element of *s2* and each element of *s2* corresponds to exactly one element of *s1* (in other words, a bijection, q.v.); equivalently, that pairing itself. Often used loosely, however, to mean a pairing such that (a) each element of *s1* corresponds to at most one element of *s2* and each element of *s2* corresponds to exactly one element of *s1,* or (b) each element of *s1* corresponds to exactly one element of *s2* and each element of *s2* corresponds to at most one element of *s1,* or (c) each element of *s1* corresponds to at most one element of *s2* and each element of *s2* corresponds to at most one element of *s1.* The term is best avoided unless the intended meaning is clear.

Example (*strict sense only*): Let *s* be the set of all integers. Then the pairing of elements *x* with their successors *x*+1 is a one-to-one correspondence from *s* to itself; so too is the pairing of elements *x* with their predecessors *x*-1.

onto (*Of a function; used as an adjective*) Having range equal to the codomain (*contrast* into). *See* bijection; surjection.

OO Object-oriented or object orientation, as the context demands.

open WFF A WFF that isn't closed; that is, a WFF that denotes a predicate that isn't a proposition.

Open World Assumption, The Loosely, the assumption that everything stated or implied by the database is true and everything else is unknown. More precisely, The Open World Assumption (OWA)—usually rejected in favor of The Closed World Assumption, q.v.—states that (a) if a given tuple appears in a given relvar at a given time, then the proposition represented by that tuple is true at that time, and (b) if a given tuple could appear in that relvar at that time but doesn't, then the proposition represented by that tuple might or might not be true at that time. At any given time, in other words, the relvar contains all and only those tuples that are known to correspond to true propositions—that is, invocations, or full instantiations, of the relvar predicate that are known to evaluate to TRUE—at that time. *Note*: The relvar in question doesn't have to be a base relvar, which is why the phrase "or implied" appears in the original loose characterization. Note too that the definition is phrased in terms of a relvar specifically, but a precisely analogous definition applies to relations also (*see* extension, third definition). Note finally that the OWA is strongly contraindicated, because it seems to lead directly to a need to support three-valued logic, q.v.

operand Something on which an operation is performed. *See also* argument; parameter.

operation An operator; sometimes, the process performed when an operator is invoked.

operator Either a read-only operator or an update operator. *Note*: The term is often used, more specifically but a trifle loosely, to mean a read-only operator in particular. It's also often used even more specifically to mean a read-only operator that's denoted by some special symbol such as "/" instead of by an identifier such as DIV, in which case other read-only operators (i.e., those denoted by identifiers) are typically referred to as functions. However, this latter usage is misleading, and hence deprecated, because all read-only operators are functions, strictly speaking.

optimization The process of converting relational expressions—in effect, queries, updates, and constraints—into the "best possible" executable code, where "best possible" basically means *best performing*. The term is somewhat of an overclaim, since it can rarely be guaranteed that the executable code produced is truly optimal in any sense. *See also* database statistics; expression transformation; semantic optimization.

optimizer The part of the DBMS responsible for optimization, q.v.

optional participation *See* cardinality constraint.

OR *See* disjunction. *Note*: OR as conventionally understood is a logical operator; however, the algebra **A**, q.v., includes an operator called OR that—by definition—is an algebraic operator (in fact, it's a generalized form of union).

ORDER BY *See* ordering.

ordered *n*-tuple *See* ordered pair. Note that an ordered *n*-tuple is not a tuple in the relational model sense (tuples in the relational model have no ordering to their components).

ordered pair A combination, usually denoted $<x,y>$, of exactly two elements x and y such that x is the first element and y the second. The ordered pairs $<x1,y1>$ and $<x2,y2>$ are equal if and only if $x1 = x2$ and $y1 = y2$ (thus $<x,y> \neq <y,x>$, in general). Formally, $<x,y>$ is defined to be equal to the set $\{\{x\},\{x,y\}\}$; observe that one of the elements in this set determines the elements that constitute the ordered pair and the other determines which of those elements comes first. *Note*: This definition can easily be extended to ordered triples, ordered quadruples, . . ., and more generally ordered *n*-tuples for any $n > 1$.

ordered tuple *See* ordered *n*-tuple.

ordering The process, or the result of the process, of imposing a left-to-right sequence on the attributes—and, more particularly, a top-to-bottom sequence on the tuples—of a relation, so that the data in the relation in question can be transferred out of the relational context and into an environment that relies on such sequences. Operators that request such sequencing, or ordering, are of major pragmatic importance, but they aren't relational operators because their result isn't a relation. *Note*: A convenient way to think of such operators is as ones that convert relations to tables (given that tables, unlike relations, do have a left-to-right ordering to their columns and a top-to-bottom ordering to their rows).

Example: The SQL operators that provide this functionality are SELECT (for left-to-right column sequence) and ORDER BY (for top-to-bottom row sequence).

Note: It's worth pointing out in passing that ORDER BY isn't a function— that is, the result of a given ORDER BY invocation is indeterminate, in general (consider, e.g., the effect of ORDER BY CITY on the relation that's the current value of relvar S as shown in Figure 1). By contrast, the operators of the relational algebra are indeed all functions. (The same can't always be said of the SQL analogs of those operators, incidentally, owing to the fact that SQL allows comparisons of the form $v1 = v2$ to return TRUE even if $v1$ and $v2$ aren't the same value.)

ORDER BY is unusual in another respect also. To be specific, it produces a sequence of tuples as its result, and yet the operators "<"and ">" are explicitly not defined for tuples (*see* tuple comparison).

ordering (mathematics) *See* partial ordering; total ordering.

ordinal type A type for which a total ordering, q.v., is defined. Let T be such a type. In general, then, the following operators will be provided in connection with type T: (a) niladic FIRST and LAST operators, which return the first value and the last value, respectively, of type T with respect to that total ordering; (b) monadic NEXT and PRIOR operators, which, given a value v of type T, return the value of type T immediately succeeding v and the value of type T immediately preceding v, respectively, again with respect to that total ordering.

Examples: Type INTEGER is an ordinal type. The NEXT and PRIOR operators are basically just "add one" and "subtract one," respectively. FIRST and LAST operators typically aren't supported directly, but selector invocations that return the minimum and maximum integers will suffice.

By way of a counterexample, suppose the system also supports a type POINT, perhaps user defined, representing geometric points in two-dimensional space. Then type POINT presumably wouldn't be an ordinal type, because the notion of one point being somehow less or greater than another makes no sense.

orthogonal Independent.

orthogonal decomposition A decomposition of some given relvar into restrictions, such that the restrictions in question satisfy The Principle of Orthogonal Design.

Examples: Suppose we were to replace relvar P by two relvars LP and HP, LP containing tuples for parts with weight less than or equal to 17.0 and HP containing tuples for parts with weight greater than 17.0; then that decomposition would be orthogonal. By contrast, suppose relvar HP were defined to contain tuples for parts with weight greater than *or equal to* 17.0; then the decomposition wouldn't be orthogonal, because tuples for parts with weight equal to 17.0 would logically belong to both LP and HP.

Orthogonal Design Principle, The *See* Principle of Orthogonal Design, The.

overloading Using the same name for two or more different operators. The operators in question should preferably have similar semantics. *Note*: Overloading is also referred to more specifically as overloading polymorphism; it's also known as ad hoc polymorphism. In an inheritance context, the term is also sometimes used to mean inclusion polymorphism, q.v.; this particular usage is deprecated, however, because it's based on a flawed perception of the nature of subtypes and supertypes. Further details are beyond the scope of this dictionary.

Examples: UNION is overloaded, because it—the name, that is—is used to mean both relational and tuple union (and in SQL it's also used to mean union plus, though oddly enough not bag union per se). Likewise, "=" is overloaded, because it applies to values of every type (i.e., there's an "=" operator for integers, another for supplier numbers, another for relations of type RELATION {S# S#, P# P#, QTY QTY}, and so on).

overriding Replacing an operator by another with the same name, same number of parameters, and same parameter and result types—that is, the same signature, q.v.—but different semantics. (It has nothing to do with domain check override, q.v.) *Contrast* overloading.

Example: Suppose there exists an operator called LOG (possibly built in) that returns natural logarithms. Then it might be possible to override that operator by one that returns logarithms to base ten instead.

OWA The Open World Assumption.

P

P-relation *See* RM/T.

pair Either a set of cardinality two or, more usually, an ordered pair (q.v.), as the context demands.

parameter A formal operand in terms of which some operator is defined, to be replaced by some argument when the operator in question is invoked. Simplifying slightly (*see* generic operator), every parameter is declared to be of some type, and any argument corresponding to a given parameter is required to be of the same type as that parameter. *Contrast* argument.

parent / parent table Deprecated, because inappropriate, terms sometimes used in SQL contexts to mean (the SQL analog of) a referenced relvar, q.v.

partial function Let f be a function with domain d and let dd be a superset of d; then f can be regarded as a partial function with domain dd. In other words, a partial function is a function, q.v., except that there can exist elements x of the domain that have no image y in the codomain. *Contrast* total function.

Example: Let s be the set of real numbers. Then "reciprocal of" is a partial function with domain and codomain both s (it's partial because there's one element of s, namely 0, that has no reciprocal).

partial instantiation *See* instantiation.

partial ordering Let s be a set. Then a partial ordering on s is a dyadic truth valued operator, usually denoted "$\leq$", such that for all x, y, and z in s, (a) $x \leq y$ or $y \leq x$ (or both, or possibly neither); (b) $x \leq x$ (reflexivity); (c) if $x \leq y$ and $y \leq z$, then $x \leq z$ (transitivity); and (d) if $x \leq y$ and $y \leq x$, then $x = y$ (antisymmetry). *Contrast* total ordering.

Example: Let *s* be an arbitrary set, let *p* be the power set of *s,* and let "≤" denote the set inclusion operator (more usually written "⊆"). Then "≤" is a partial ordering on *p*. (Moreover, it's a partial ordering that isn't a total ordering, except in the degenerate case in which the cardinality of *s* is either zero or one.)

partitioning Let *s* be a set. Then a partitioning of *s* is a set of subsets ("partitions") of *s* such that every element of *s* is an element of exactly one such subset. Note that (a) partitions are pairwise disjoint; (b) their union is equal to *s*. *See also* equivalence class.

Peirce arrow *See* NOR.

persistence The property according to which data, once inserted into the database, remains there ("persists") until explicitly deleted. Base relvars in particular are persistent in this sense.

physical data independence *See* data independence.

physical database design The process (or the result of the process) of deciding, given some logical database design, how that logical design should map to whatever physical structures the target DBMS happens to support. Note, therefore, that the physical design should be derived from the logical design and not the other way around; ideally, in fact, it should be derived automatically.

picture (*Of a relation, attribute, or tuple*) *See* table, column, and row, respectively; *see also* cell. Note in all cases that there's a logical difference between the picture and the thing pictured.

pipelining An implementation technique in which tuples of an intermediate result relation are produced and passed on to another operation one at a time instead of en bloc. *Contrast* materialization (first definition).

PJ/NF Projection-join normal form, q.v.

placeholder A free variable or parameter.

PNF Prenex normal form.

pointer An implementation construct. As is well known, pointers are excluded from the relational model. In fact, mixing pointers and relations—that is, allowing a "relation" to have an "attribute" whose values are pointers to "tuples" in some other "relation" (a state of affairs supported by several SQL products as well as by the SQL standard, despite the fact that it violates The Information Principle among other things)—has been described as The Second Great Blunder. (For the first, *see* type.) *See also* referencing. *Note*: Some writers reserve the term *pointer* to mean, specifically, one whose value is some kind of physical address, using the term *reference* (or some such term) for other kinds of pointers. This distinction might be useful in certain contexts but is irrelevant to the relational model. Note too that foreign keys in particular aren't pointers; among other things, foreign key values identify tuples, which are values, whereas pointer values are addresses and therefore, by definition, identify variables (that's why they violate The Information Principle). *See* value; variable.

polymorphic operator *See* polymorphism.

polymorphism Loosely, the idea that an operator might permit its arguments to be of different types on different invocations. *See* generic polymorphism; inclusion polymorphism; overloading.

positive Strictly greater than zero. *Contrast* nonnegative.

power set The set of all subsets of a given set. If the given set has cardinality n, the power set has cardinality 2^n (this count includes both the empty set and the set that's identical to the original set, both of which are indeed subsets of the original set).

predicate A truth valued function. Given an arbitrary predicate, substituting arguments for the parameters of that predicate yields a proposition (thus, another way of thinking about a predicate is as a parameterized or generalized proposition). *Note*: If and only if that set of parameters is empty, the predicate degenerates to a proposition (i.e., it already is a proposition). In other words, all propositions are predicates, but most predicates aren't propositions.

predicate calculus A sound and complete formal system having to do with predicates and connectives and the inferences that can be made using such predicates and connectives. *Note*: The principal difference between predicate calculus and propositional calculus, q.v., is that predicates, unlike propositions, are allowed to contain quantifiers and logic variables (both free and bound), which makes predicate calculus more powerful and more widely applicable.

predicate constant Same as predicate.

predicate expression An expression denoting a predicate; that is, an expression involving predicate constants, predicate variables, connectives, and parentheses. *Note*: Few logic texts if any actually use this term; in fact, logic texts in general don't seem to have a term for the construct at all other than *predicate* itself (not even ones that use *propositional form* for a propositional expression, which might be expected to use the surely obvious *predicate form* for a predicate expression).

Examples: If p and q are predicate variables, then p, q, the conjunction (p) AND (q), the disjunction (p) OR (q), and the negation NOT(p) are all predicate expressions.

predicate form Same as predicate expression.

predicate logic Same as predicate calculus.

predicate variable A variable whose value is a predicate. (Some writers use the term to mean a free variable, but this usage is deprecated.)

premise / premiss In logic, something assumed to be true for the purposes of a proof or attempted proof.

prenex normal form A predicate is in prenex normal form (PNF) if and only if all of the quantifiers appear at the beginning; more precisely, it's in PNF if and only if (a) it's quantifier free or (b) it's of the form EXISTS x (p) or FORALL x (p), where p is in PNF in turn. Thus, a PNF predicate takes the form

```
Q1 x1 ( Q2 x2  ( ... ( Qn xn ( p ) ) ... ) )
```

where (a) $n \geq 0$, (b) each Qi ($i = 1,2, \ldots , n$) is either EXISTS or FORALL, and (c) the predicate p—which is sometimes called the matrix—is quantifier free.

Example: Consider the following tuple calculus query ("Get suppliers who supply at least one red part"):

```
SX   RANGES OVER { S }  ;
SPX  RANGES OVER { SP } ;
PX   RANGES OVER { P }  ;

SX WHERE
EXISTS PX ( PX.COLOR = 'Red' AND
              EXISTS SPX ( SPX.S# = SX.S# AND
                           SPX.P# = PX.P# ) )
```

The predicate in the WHERE clause here is not in prenex normal form. Here, however, is a semantically equivalent formulation of the query in which the predicate is in prenex normal form:

```
SX WHERE
EXISTS PX ( EXISTS SPX ( PX.COLOR = 'Red' AND
                         SPX.S# = SX.S# AND
                         SPX.P# = PX.P# ) )
```

Prenex normal form is no more logically correct than any other, but with a little practice it does tend to become the easiest to write.

preserving dependencies *See* FD preservation.

primary domain Let R be a base relvar; let R have a primary key, K; let K be simple (*see* simple key); and let K be defined on domain (i.e., type) D. Then, and only then, D is a primary domain. *Note*: Since (a) it clearly violates The Principle of Interchangeability and (b) it relies on a concept, primary key, that's hard to justify from a logical point of view (*see* primary key), the primary domain concept is strongly deprecated. In any case, the term (perhaps fortunately) isn't much used; we mention it here mainly for historical reasons.

Examples: In the case of the suppliers-and-parts database, the sole primary domains are S# and P#.

primary key A candidate key that has been singled out for special syntactic treatment for some reason. While a given relvar can have any number of candidate keys, it can have at most one primary key. For a given relvar, however, whether some candidate key is to be chosen as primary, and if so which one, are essentially psychological issues, beyond the purview of the relational model as such. *Note*: The relational model originally insisted that base relvars, at least, should always have a primary key. It also insisted that foreign keys reference primary keys specifically. However, there were never any good logical reasons for these rules, and in any case rules that apply to base relvars but not other kinds are more than a little suspect anyway (because they violate The Principle of Interchangeability); thus, the primary key notion could be dropped without serious loss. We mention it here mainly for historical reasons.

prime attribute Old fashioned and somewhat deprecated term for a key attribute (not necessarily a primary key attribute).

primitive operator Loosely, an operator not defined in terms of others. More precisely, let s be a set of operators. Let Op be an operator in s that can be defined in terms of other operators in s; remove Op from s, and repeat this step until it can't be repeated any more. What remains is a set of operators that are primitive with respect to s. Note that the set of primitive operators with respect to a given set s is not necessarily unique.

Examples: 1. For relational algebra, a primitive set of operators (a) will definitely include projection, (b) will probably include join, but (c) will probably not include semijoin (because semijoin can be defined in terms of projection and join). *See* **A**. 2. For two-valued logic, any of the following sets of operators can be taken as primitive: {NOT,OR}; {NOT,AND}; {NOR}; {NAND}.

Principle of Cautious Design, The A guiding principle in the design of formal systems (including databases, DBMSs, database languages, and many others). It can be stated thus: given a design choice between options *A* and *B,* where *A* is upward compatible with *B* and the full implications of *B* aren't yet known, the cautious decision is to go with *A*. Going with *A* permits future "opening up" of the design to *B* if such opening up becomes desirable. By contrast, going with *B* prohibits future "closing down" of the design to *A,* even if such closing down becomes desirable (i.e., if it becomes clear that *B* was a bad decision in the first place).

Example: The designers of SQL had a choice between prohibiting duplicate rows (*Option A*) and permitting them (*Option B*). The cautious decision would have been to prohibit them (*Option A*); they could then have been supported in the future, if a clear need for such support were ever demonstrated. Unfortunately, the designers chose to permit them (*Option B*). Of course, this decision turned out to be a very bad one, but now there's no compatible way for SQL to go back to *Option A*. *Note*: As this example suggests, The Principle of Cautious Design can help to avoid situations in which the language (or the DBMS, or the database, or whatever else it is that's being designed) provides certain options that users have to be explicitly told not to exercise.

Principle of Identity of Indiscernibles, The The principle that if there's no way whatsoever of distinguishing between two objects, then there aren't two objects but only one. Or equivalently: every object has its own unique identity. *Note*: In the relational model, such unique identities are represented in the same way as everything else—namely, by means of attribute values (*see* Information Principle, The)—and numerous benefits accrue from this fact. Note too that there's a logical difference between indiscernibility and interchangeability—two objects might be interchangeable and yet distinguishable (think of two pennies, for example). Note finally that the term *object* is not being used here in its OO sense.

Principle of Incoherence, The A principle, sometimes invoked in defense of a less than fully successful attempt at criticizing some technical issue, to the effect that it's hard to criticize something coherently if what's being criticized is itself not very coherent in the first place. Occasionally referred to, a little unkindly, as The Incoherent Principle.

Principle of Interchangeability, The See Interchangeability Principle, The.

Principles of Normalization, The *See* normalization principles.

Principle of Orthogonal Design, The Loosely, the principle that no two relvars in a given database should have overlapping meanings. More precisely, let A and B be distinct relvars. Replace A and B by nonloss decompositions into projections $A1, A2, \ldots, Am$ and $B1, B2, \ldots, Bn,$ respectively, such that every Ai ($i = 1, 2, \ldots, m$) and every Bj ($j = 1, 2, \ldots, n$) is in 6NF. Let some i and j be such that there exists a sequence of zero or more attribute renamings with the property that
(a) when applied to $Ai,$ it produces $Ak,$ and (b) Ak and Bj are of the same type. Then there must not exist a constraint to the effect that, at all times, (Ak WHERE ax) = (Bj WHERE bx), where ax and bx are restriction conditions, q.v., neither of which is a contradiction, q.v.

Principle of Uniform Representation, The *See* Information Principle, The.

Principle of Uniformity of Representation, The *See* Information Principle, The.

product Cartesian product, q.v. (unless the context demands otherwise).

product (bag theory) *See* bag.

product (set theory) *See* Cartesian product (set theory).

projection Let *r* be a relation and let {*X*} be a subset of the heading of *r*. Then the projection of *r* on {*X*}, *r*{*X*}, is a relation with heading {*X*} and body consisting of all tuples *x* such that there exists some tuple *t* in *r* with *X* value *x*. *See also* tuple projection.

Example: The expression S{STATUS,CITY} denotes a projection of the relation that's the current value of relvar S. That projection is a relation of type RELATION {STATUS INTEGER, CITY CHAR}, containing all possible tuples of the form <*st,sc*> (and no other tuples) such that there exists some supplier number *s#* and some name *sn* such that the tuple <*s#,sn,st,sc*> appears in the current value of relvar S. Given the sample values of Figure 1, the result has cardinality four. *Note*: For reasons of user friendliness, **Tutorial D** allows projections to be expressed in terms of the attributes to be removed instead of those to be retained; thus, for example, the projection S{STATUS,CITY} can equivalently be expressed as S{ALL BUT S#,SNAME}. A similar remark applies to several other **Tutorial D** constructs also—KEY, GROUP, SUMMARIZE, and so on.

projection-join normal form Fifth normal form. The alternative, and original, name *projection-join normal form* derives from the fact that 5NF is "the" normal form with respect to projection and join, as those operators are classically understood.

proof (*Logic*) In general, a sequence of sentences in some logical system that together establish some sentence as a logical consequence of certain given sentences; if the given sentences are true, then the consequential sentence is also true. A direct proof is a sequence in which each sentence is either an axiom or can be deduced from previous sentences in the sequence by means of the rules of inference of the system; the final sentence is a theorem. An axiom is a theorem with a single-sentence direct proof. An indirect proof, also known as a *reductio ad absurdum* proof, is a sequence of sentences that together establish some sentence as a theorem by showing that its negation leads to a contradiction.

propagating updates *See* controlled redundancy.

proper inclusion Set $s1$ properly includes set $s2$ ("$s1 \supset s2$") if and only if it is a proper superset of $s2$; set $s2$ is properly included in set $s1$ ("$s2 \subset s1$") if and only if it is a proper subset of $s1$.

proper subkey A subkey that isn't a key (i.e., a proper subset of a key).

proper subset Set $s2$ is a proper subset of set $s1$ ("$s2 \subset s1$") if and only if it is a subset of $s1$ and $s1$ and $s2$ are distinct.

proper superkey A superkey that isn't a key (i.e., a superkey that doesn't have the irreducibility property); loosely, a proper superset of a key.

proper superset Set $s1$ is a proper superset of set $s2$ ("$s1 \supset s2$") if and only if it is a superset of $s2$ and $s1$ and $s2$ are distinct.

property A thing belonging to another thing. *Note*: It's frequently suggested that there should be a one-to-one correspondence between "properties of interest" and attributes in base relvars. The suggestion is hard to sustain, however, given that the term *properties of interest* has no precise definition. (Of course, the same is true of the term *property* itself, come to that.)

proposition A 0-place predicate; a predicate with no parameters (i.e., no free variables); a declarative statement (in the sense of logic, not the programming language sense); hence, something that evaluates unequivocally to either TRUE or FALSE. *Note*: Strictly speaking, if *S* is a declarative statement, the corresponding proposition isn't really *S* as such—rather, it's the assertion made by *S*. For example, consider the statements "The sun is a star" and *"Le soleil est une étoile."* Clearly, there are two distinct statements here; however, they both denote the same proposition. However, it's usual to ignore this fine distinction in informal contexts (and sometimes in more formal contexts as well).

Examples: 1. The sun is a star. 2. Neptune is a star. 3. All politicians are corrupt. 4. Supplier S1 is under contract, is named Smith, has status 20, and is located in Paris. 5. There exists a city *c* such that there exists a supplier number *s#* such that the supplier with supplier number *s#* is located in city *c*. Notice that there are two variables, *s#* and *c*, in this last example; however, the variables in question are bound, not free, and the example overall still evaluates unequivocally to either TRUE or FALSE (it's either the case or not the case that at least one supplier is located in at least one city). 6. Let *p* be an arbitrary predicate. If every parameter of *p* is either quantified or replaced by some argument, then what results is a proposition. For example, given the predicate "The supplier with supplier number *s#* is named *sn,* has status *st,* and is located in city *sc,*" the statement "There exists a city *sc* such that there exists a supplier number *s#* such that the supplier with supplier number *s#* is named Smith, has status 20, and is located in city *sc*" is a proposition. 7. By way of a counterexample, the expression "*x* > 0 OR TRUE" is not a proposition (because it involves a parameter, *x*), even though it does evaluate unequivocally to TRUE. In other words, although propositions always evaluate unequivocally to either TRUE or FALSE, not everything that evaluates unequivocally to either TRUE or FALSE is a proposition.
In fact, a useful informal test for checking whether some statement *S* is a proposition is the following: *S* is a proposition if and only if "Is it the case that *S*?" is a well formed question in natural language.

propositional calculus A sound, complete, and decidable formal system having to do with propositions and connectives and the inferences that can be made using such propositions and connectives. *Contrast* predicate calculus.

propositional constant Same as proposition.

propositional expression An expression denoting a proposition; that is, an expression involving propositional constants, propositional variables, connectives, and parentheses. *Note*: Logic texts don't use this term much, typically preferring the term *propositional form,* q.v. (if they use any term for the concept at all, that is).

Examples: If p and q are propositional variables, then p, q, the conjunction (p) AND (q), the disjunction (p) OR (q), and the negation NOT(p) are all propositional expressions.

propositional form Same as propositional expression.

propositional function Same as predicate.

propositional logic Same as propositional calculus.

propositional variable A variable whose value is a proposition and is thus, effectively, either TRUE or FALSE. (Some writers use the term to mean a free variable, but this usage is deprecated.)

proto tuple Loosely, the portion of a relational calculus expression that precedes the WHERE clause. The term is shorthand for "prototype tuple"; it's useful but nonstandard.

pseudovariable reference The use of an operational expression instead of a simple variable reference to denote the target for some update operation. *Note*: It's convenient for definitional purposes to regard pseudovariable references as if they were regular variable references (and we do so in this dictionary); in other words, pseudovariables are variables, loosely speaking.

Examples: Let CS be a variable of type CHAR, with current value the string 'Middle', and consider the following assignment:

```
SUBSTR ( CS, 2, 1 ) = 'u' ;
```

SUBSTR here is the substring operator, and the effect of the assignment is to "zap" the second character position within CS, replacing the 'i' with a 'u' (after the update, therefore, the current value of CS is the string 'Muddle'). The expression on the left side of the assignment is a pseudovariable reference.

For a second example, let LSV be a view, defined as the restriction of relvar S to just suppliers in London, and consider the following DELETE statement:

```
DELETE LSV WHERE STATUS > 15 ;
```

Logically speaking, this DELETE is equivalent to the following:

```
DELETE ( S WHERE CITY = 'London' )
          WHERE STATUS > 15 ;
```

In this expanded form, the target of the DELETE is specified as an operational expression (i.e., a pseudovariable reference). As the example suggests, therefore, updating a view is logically equivalent to updating a certain pseudovariable (thus, views are pseudovariables, loosely speaking).

Q

QBE A relational language based on domain calculus. The name is an abbreviation for Query-By-Example.

quantification Applying a quantifier (q.v.) to a free variable, thereby converting that free variable into a bound variable (*see* binding) and converting the predicate containing that free variable into a different predicate, logically distinct from the original. *Note*: If every free variable in the original predicate is quantified in this way, what results is a proposition.

quantifier *See* existential quantifier; universal quantifier. *Note*: Other quantifiers are possible—for example, there exists exactly one of (*see* UNIQUE); for all but one of; there exists an odd number of; and so on— but EXISTS and FORALL are easily the ones most frequently encountered in practice.

QUEL A relational language based on tuple calculus that at one time was a serious competitor to SQL.

query A retrieval request (i.e., a relational expression, or a statement that asks for the evaluation of such an expression). Sometimes used, loosely, to refer to update requests also; also used to refer to the informal natural language counterpart to some retrieval or update request.

query decomposition A divide and conquer technique for evaluating relational expressions by recursively dividing them into subexpressions.

query rewrite *See* expression transformation.

quota query A query that imposes a desired limit, or quota, on the cardinality of the result.

Example: Here's a possible formulation of the quota query "Get the three heaviest parts" (the quota here is three):

```
WITH ( P RENAME ( WEIGHT AS WT ) ) AS t1 ,
     ( EXTEND P ADD ( COUNT ( t1 WHERE WT > WEIGHT )
                       AS #_HEAVIER ) AS t2 ,
     ( t2 WHERE #_HEAVIER < 3 ) AS t3 :
  t3 { P#, PNAME, WEIGHT, COLOR, CITY }
```

Using the RANK shorthand, q.v., we can express this query a little more succinctly thus:

```
( ( RANK P BY ( DESC WEIGHT AS W ) ) WHERE W ≤ 3 )
                  { P#, PNAME, WEIGHT, COLOR, CITY }
```

Note that the cardinality of the result of a given quota query might not be exactly equal to the specified quota; in fact, it might be either less than or greater than that quota, depending on the query itself and also on the relations involved in that query.

R

range 1. *See* function. 2. *See* range variable.

range variable Relational calculus analog of a logic variable; in other words, a variable that "ranges over" some specified set of values—either the set of tuples in some relation (in tuple calculus) or the set of values of some type (in domain calculus)—and can appear either bound or free in relational calculus expressions.

Examples: See the examples under domain calculus and tuple calculus.

RANK *See* ranking.

ranking Let r be a relation with no attribute called X. Then the ranking RANK r BY (*item, . . ., item* AS X), where each *item* consists of either ASC (ascending) or DESC (descending) followed by an attribute reference identifying an attribute of r (and the overall sequence of items specifies major-to-minor ordering in the usual way), is a relation identical to r except that (a) it has an additional attribute X and (b) the X value in any given tuple of that result shows that tuple's ranking position with respect to the specified ordering.

Example: See quota query.

read-only operator A function; i.e., an operator that, when invoked, updates nothing (except possibly variables local to the implementation of the operator in question) but returns a value, of a type declared when the operator in question is defined. A read-only operator invocation thus denotes a value; i.e., it's an expression—by definition, in fact, every expression is a read-only operator invocation (*see* expression)—and it can appear wherever a literal of the appropriate type is allowed. In particular, it can be nested inside other expressions. *Note*: As mentioned elsewhere in this dictionary, certain SQL read-only operators in particular are "possibly nondeterministic," meaning they're not functions at all, technically speaking. In truth, they really are functions; however, they're ones that are deliberately underspecified and thus don't behave like functions from the user's point of view.

Example: See the first example under argument.

real relation The value of a given real relvar at a given time.

real relvar A base relvar or a snapshot (*contrast* virtual relvar).

record Term sometimes used to mean a row, in any of the possible senses of that term. All such uses are deprecated, however; the term is better reserved for an operating system or even physical level construct.

recursive query A relational expression—which by definition can be thought of as the invocation of some relation valued operator *Op*—whose evaluation involves further invocations of that same operator *Op*.

Example: Here's a recursive definition of an operator to compute the transitive closure, q.v., of a binary relation with attributes A and B, both of type P# (the code isn't very efficient, but it can obviously be improved in a variety of ways):

```
OPERATOR TRANCLO ( AB RELATION { A P#, B P# } )
                RETURNS RELATION { A P#, B P# } ;
   RETURN
 ( WITH ( AB UNION
          ( ( AB RENAME ( B AS C ) ) COMPOSE
            ( AB RENAME ( A AS C ) ) ) AS ttt :
         IF ttt = AB THEN ttt ELSE TRANCLO ( ttt )
         END IF ) ;
 END OPERATOR ;
```

Now the invocation TRANCLO(*r*), where *r* is a relation of the appropriate type, can be thought of as a recursive query, because its evaluation involves further invocations of TRANCLO itself (in general).

recursive relationship A relationship (in the sense of the third definition of that term, q.v.) in which the two sets participating are one and the same. The term isn't particularly apt, since there's no recursion, as such, involved.

reductio ad absurdum "Reduction to absurdity"; a method of proof, q.v., that establishes something as true by showing that its negation leads to a contradiction.

redundancy A database displays redundancy if and only if it contains, directly or indirectly, two or more distinct representations of the same proposition. *See also* controlled redundancy.

referenced key *See* foreign key.

referenced relvar *See* foreign key.

referenced tuple *See* foreign key.

referencing The relational meaning of this term is as described under foreign key; it should not be confused with the operator of the same name—found in systems that support pointers but not in relational systems—that, given a variable V, returns a pointer to V. *Note*: Systems that support pointers usually support an operator called *dereferencing* as well, which, given a pointer p, returns the variable V that p points to.

referencing relvar *See* foreign key.

referencing tuple *See* foreign key.

referential action The action specification portion of a foreign key rule (e.g., "cascade," in a DELETE rule); also used to mean the specified action as such.

referential constraint *See* foreign key.

referential cycle A referential path, q.v., from some relvar to itself. Database designs involving such cycles are usually contraindicated.

referential integrity Loosely, the rule that no referencing tuple is allowed to exist if the corresponding referenced tuple doesn't exist. More precisely, let *FK* be some foreign key in some referencing relvar *R2*; let *K* be the corresponding key in the corresponding referenced relvar *R1*; and let *K'* be derived from *K* as explained under foreign key. Then the referential integrity rule requires there never to be a time at which there exists an *FK* value in *R2* that isn't the *K'* value for some (necessarily unique) tuple in *R1*. *See also* foreign key; foreign key rule.

referential path Let relvars *Rz, Ry, Rx, . . ., Rb, Ra* be such that there exists a referential constraint from *Rz* to *Ry*, a referential constraint from *Ry* to *Rx, . . .*, and a referential constraint from *Rb* to *Ra*. Then the chain of such constraints from *Rz* to *Ra* constitutes a referential path from *Rz* to *Ra* (and the number of constraints in the chain is the length of the path).

reflexivity 1. (*Of a dyadic logical operator*) The dyadic logical operator *Op*, which we assume for definiteness is expressed in infix style, is reflexive if and only if, for all *x, x Op x* is true. 2. (*Of a binary relation*) The binary relation *r* is reflexive if and only if, for all *x*, the tuple $\langle x,x \rangle$ appears in *r*. 3. (*Of FDs*) *See* Armstrong's inference rules. *Note*: The first two of these definitions are slightly simplified, in that they deliberately fail to specify the range of possible values for *x*.

Examples (*first definition only*): The logical operator EQUIV; the "less than or equals" operator "≤".

refresh *See* snapshot.

relation A relation value, q.v. *Note*: As is well known, the term is also commonly used to refer to a relation variable, but this usage is deprecated as the source of much confusion.

relation (mathematics) Given sets *s1, s2, . . ., sn*, not necessarily distinct, *r* is a relation on those sets if and only if it's a set of *n*-tuples each of which has its first element from *s1*, its second element from *s2*, and so on. (Equivalently, *r* is a subset of the Cartesian product *s1* × *s2* × *. . .* × *sn*.)

Set si is the ith domain of r ($i = 1, \ldots, n$). *Note*: There are several important logical differences between relations in mathematics and their relational model counterparts. Here are some of them:

- Mathematical relations have a left-to-right ordering to their attributes.

- Actually, mathematical relations have, at best, only a very rudimentary concept of attributes anyway. Certainly their attributes aren't named, other than by their ordinal position.

- As a consequence, mathematical relations don't really have either a heading or a type in the relational model sense.

- Mathematical relations are usually either binary or, just occasionally, unary. By contrast, relations in the relational model are of degree n, where n can be any nonnegative integer.

- Relational operators such as JOIN, EXTEND, and the rest were first defined in the context of the relational model specifically; the mathematical theory of relations includes few such operators.

And so on (the foregoing isn't meant to be an exhaustive list).

relation assignment Relational assignment, q.v.

relation comparison Relational comparison, q.v.

relation constant A relation, especially one that's named; not to be confused with a relation literal, q.v.

Examples: TABLE_DEE and TABLE_DUM. *Note*: These two relation constants are probably built in (assuming they're supported at all, that is, which in today's products they're probably not). Here by contrast is one that's user defined:

```
CONST STATES_OF_THE_USA
  RELATION { TUPLE { STATE NAME('Alabama') } ,
             TUPLE { STATE NAME('Alaska' ) } ,
                    . . . . . . . . . . . . .
             TUPLE { STATE NAME('Wyoming') } } } ;
```

relation equality Equality of relations; relations *r1* and *r2* are equal (i.e., the relational comparison *r1* = *r2* evaluates to TRUE) if and only if *r1* and *r2* are the very same relation.

relation expression Relational expression, q.v.

relation literal A literal that denotes a relation; not to be confused with a relation constant, q.v.

Examples: See the examples under literal.

relation inclusion Relational inclusion, q.v.

relation predicate Let *r* be a relation. Then the relation predicate for *r* is the predicate that represents the user-understood meaning of *r* in some particular context. If *r* is of degree *n,* that predicate will be *n*-adic (it will have a parameter for each attribute of *r*). Under The Closed World Assumption, moreover, the body of *r* will contain all and only those tuples that correspond to invocations of that predicate that evaluate to TRUE.

Examples: 1. Let *r* be the projection of the current value of relvar S on {S#,CITY}. Then the predicate for *r* is "There exists a name *sn* and a status *st* such that supplier S# is under contract, is named *sn*, has status *st,* and is located in CITY." Note that this predicate is dyadic, as is to be expected for a binary relation. 2. Consider the relations *r1* and *r2,* where *r1* is the projection S{CITY} and *r2* is the projection P{CITY}. Then it's certainly possible for *r1* and *r2* to be equal; nevertheless, they have different predicates, corresponding to their two different contexts (loosely speaking, the predicates are "There exists a supplier located in CITY" and "There exists a part stored in CITY," respectively).

relation schema / relation scheme Terms much used in the research literature (though very little in commercial practice) to mean a relation heading.

relation selector *See* selector.

relation type Let {*H*} be a heading; then RELATION {*H*} is a relation type with the same degree and attributes as {*H*}.

Examples: The type of relvar S is

```
RELATION { S# S#, SNAME NAME,
                  STATUS INTEGER, CITY CHAR }
```

The following (corresponding to a certain projection of relvar S) is also a relation type:

```
RELATION { CITY CHAR, SNAME NAME }
```

relation type generator *See* type generator.

relation type inference The process of determining the type of the value denoted by a given relational expression. Note that this process is completely specified by the rules defining the types of the results of the various relational operations, q.v.

relation value Loosely, a table (value). More precisely, let RELATION {*H*} be a relation type, and let {*b*} be a set of tuples of type TUPLE {*H*}. Let *r* be the pair <{*H*},{*b*}>. Then *r* is a relation value (relation for short) of type RELATION {*H*}, with heading {*H*} and body {*b*}, and the same degree and attributes as {*H*} and the same cardinality as {*b*}. *Contrast* relation variable; relvar. *Note*: It follows from this definition that a relation doesn't really contain tuples (it contains a body, and that body in turn contains tuples), but it's usual to talk as if relations contained tuples directly, for simplicity. Note too that relations in the relational model differ in certain important respects from the mathematical construct of the same name. In particular, relations in mathematics typically don't have named attributes; instead, their attributes are identified by their ordinal position, left to right. For other differences, *see* relation (mathematics).

relation valued attribute An attribute whose type is some relation type. Values of such an attribute are relations of the specified type (sometimes called nested relations, since they're "nested" inside tuples—especially tuples in some other relation). *Note*: If a relvar has a relation valued attribute, that fact in and of itself doesn't constitute a violation of any particular level of normalization (not even first); however, such attributes are usually contraindicated in base relvars, because they necessarily imply some structural asymmetry and thereby give rise to asymmetry (and complexity) in queries, constraints, and updates as well. *See also* grouping; ungrouping.

relation variable Loosely, a table (variable); more precisely, a variable whose type is some relation type. Let relation variable R be of type RELATION $\{H\}$; then R has the same heading (and therefore attributes) and degree as that type does. Let the value of R at some given time be r; then R has the same body and cardinality at that time as r does. Note that a relation variable is *not* the same thing as a set of tuple variables (not even a set of tuple variables all of the same type). *Contrast* relation; relation value.

relational algebra An open-ended collection of read-only operators on relations, each of which takes one or more relations as operands and produces a relation as a result. Exactly which operators are included is somewhat arbitrary, but the collection overall is required to be at least as powerful as relational calculus, in the sense that every relational calculus expression is semantically equivalent to some relational algebra expression. Also, the operators are generic, in the sense that they apply to all possible relations (loosely speaking). *Note*: If we want relational algebra to be regarded as an algebra in the same sense that the algebra of sets, q.v., is so regarded—which presumably we do—then we ought really to include, in addition to the operators that produce a relation as a result, a relational inclusion operator, q.v. Note further that relational assignment is also a relational operator, but it isn't a relational algebra operator because it isn't read-only.

relational assignment An operation that assigns a relation value to a relation variable (of the same type). *See* assignment.

relational calculus An applied form of predicate calculus, tailored to operating on relations, with the property that every relational calculus expression is semantically equivalent to some relational algebra expression. *See also* domain calculus; tuple calculus.

relational comparison A Boolean expression of the form (*exp1*) *theta* (*exp2*), where *exp1* and *exp2* are relational expressions of the same type *T* and *theta* is any comparison operator that makes sense for relations of type *T* (e.g., "=", "≠", "⊆"). *Note*: The parentheses surrounding *exp1* and *exp2* in the comparison might not be needed in practice.

relational completeness A measure of the expressive power of a language; essentially, a language is relationally complete if and only if it's at least as powerful as relational calculus, meaning that any relation definable by some relational calculus expression is also definable by some expression of the language in question.

Examples: Relational algebra is relationally complete, because every relational calculus expression is semantically equivalent to some relational algebra expression. (In fact the converse is true as well; that is, every relational algebra expression is semantically equivalent to some relational calculus expression, at least with the algebra and calculus as usually defined.) For example, the relational calculus expression shown as an example under tuple calculus is semantically equivalent to the relational algebra expression (S MATCHING SP){SNAME}. It follows that in order to prove that a given language *L* is relationally complete, it suffices to prove that every relational algebra expression is semantically equivalent to some expression in *L*—which is often easier than proving that every relational calculus expression is semantically equivalent to some expression in *L*. SQL, for example, can be shown to be "almost" relationally complete in this way ("almost," because SQL fails to support TABLE_DEE and TABLE_DUM). *Note*: In fact, SQL is "more than" relationally complete, in that its expressions permit the definition of many objects that aren't relations at all. As this example suggests, being more than relationally complete isn't necessarily a good thing.

relational database A database that abides by The Information Principle. We assume throughout this dictionary that all databases are relational, barring explicit statements to the contrary. *Note*: SQL databases must be regarded as only approximately relational at best, since SQL involves so many departures from The Information Principle (including but not limited to the departures identified under table).

relational DBMS A DBMS that manages relational databases (and no others); equivalently, a DBMS that implements the relational model. *Note*: SQL DBMSs must be regarded as only approximately relational at best, since SQL involves so many departures from the relational model (including but not limited to the departures identified under table).

relational expression An expression denoting a relation. Relation literals, relation selector invocations, relcon and relvar references, and relational algebra operator invocations are all special cases.

relational inclusion Let relations *r1* and *r2* be of the same type. Then *r1* includes *r2* ("$r1 \supseteq r2$") if and only if its body is a superset of that of *r2*, and *r2* is included in *r1* ("$r2 \subseteq r1$") if and only if its body is a subset of that of *r1*. Relation *r1* is equal to relation *r2* ("$r1 = r2$") if and only if each includes the other. Observe that every relation is included in itself, also that every relation includes the empty relation of the applicable type. Observe also that the term *relational inclusion* is usually taken, a trifle arbitrarily, to refer to the "$\subseteq$" operator specifically, not the "$\supseteq$" operator.

relational model The formal theory or foundation on which relational databases in particular and relational technology in general are based. The relational model is often loosely characterized as having three aspects: a structural aspect, which has to do with relations per se; an integrity aspect, which has to do with candidate and foreign keys; and a manipulative aspect, which has to do with operators such as join. More precisely, the relational model consists of the following components: (a) an open-ended collection of scalar types, including in particular type BOOLEAN; (b) a relation type generator and an intended interpretation for relations of types generated thereby; (c) facilities for defining relation variables of such generated relation types; (d) a relational assignment operator; and (e) an open-ended collection of generic read-only operators (i.e., relational algebra or relational calculus) for deriving relations from relations. Note part (e) in particular; it's a far too common error to regard the relational model as consisting of structure only and to overlook the operators, and yet (as Codd once said) structure without operators is rather like anatomy without physiology. Note moreover that those operators aren't just meant for writing queries, as many seem to think; rather, they're for writing expressions, expressions that serve many purposes, including query but not limited to query alone. One particularly important purpose is the formulation of constraints (though in this case the relational expression will be just a subexpression of some Boolean expression, frequently though not invariably an invocation of IS_EMPTY, q.v.). *Note:* In the interest of physical data independence, the relational model is deliberately silent on everything to do with performance (including physical storage representations in particular).

relational operator An operator that (a) takes either relations or relvars (or both) as operands and (b) either returns a relation or updates at least one relvar.

relationship 1. A term used briefly in Codd's early papers (later discarded) to mean what we would now call either a relation or a relvar, as the context demands. 2. In E/R modeling, "an association among entities" (definition taken from Chen's original E/R paper). 3. More generally, given two sets (not necessarily distinct), a rule pairing elements of the first set with elements of the second set; equivalently, that pairing itself. This definition can easily be extended to three, four, or any number of given sets (e.g., consider the relationship involving suppliers, parts, and projects mentioned in the example under fifth normal form).

relative complement *See* complement (set theory).

relcon A relation constant, q.v.

relcon reference Syntactically, a relcon name, used to denote the value of that relcon.

relvar A relation variable, q.v. *Note*: For simplicity, we assume in this dictionary that all relvars are part of some database ("database relvars"). However, there's no good reason why relvars that are local to some application ("application relvars") shouldn't be supported as well.

relvar constraint 1. (*"A" relvar constraint*) Formally, any constraint that refers to the relvar in question, as well as possibly to others; informally, a single-relvar constraint, q.v. *Note*: These two definitions aren't meant to be equivalent in any sense—they refer to two distinct concepts.
2. (*"The" relvar constraint*) The logical AND of TRUE and all constraints, apart from type constraints, that apply to a given relvar (*the* relvar constraint—sometimes called the *total* relvar constraint—for the relvar in question); in other words, the formal, system-understood "meaning" for the relvar in question (*contrast* relvar predicate). Note that it follows from this definition that every relvar is subject to at least one constraint: namely, the degenerate ("default") constraint TRUE. Note too that all relvar constraints, in either sense, are also database constraints, q.v.

Examples: First, the key constraint specified in the definition of relvar S is a relvar constraint on that relvar. Second, the foreign key constraint from SP to S is a relvar constraint for both relvar S and relvar SP. Third, here are some more relvar constraints (repeated from the examples under database constraint) that might apply to relvar S:

```
CONSTRAINT C1 IS_EMPTY
   ( S WHERE STATUS < 1 OR STATUS > 100 ) ;
/* status values must be in the */
/* range 1 to 100 inclusive    */


CONSTRAINT C3 IS_EMPTY
   ( ( S JOIN SP )
     WHERE STATUS < 20 AND P# = P#('P6') ) ;
/* no supplier with status less */
/* than 20 can supply part P6   */
```

(Constraint C3 is also a relvar constraint for relvar SP.)

Finally, suppose for the sake of the example that the foregoing constraints (the key constraint on relvar S, the foreign key constraint from relvar SP to relvar S, and constraints C1 and C3 above) are the only ones that apply to relvar S. Then the logical AND of all of them and TRUE is "the" (total) relvar constraint for that relvar.

relvar predicate Let R be a relvar (real or virtual). Then the relvar predicate for R is the predicate that represents the user-understood meaning of R. If R is of degree n, that predicate will be n-adic (it will have a parameter for each attribute of R). Under The Closed World Assumption, moreover, at any given time the body of R will contain all and only those tuples that correspond to invocations of that predicate that evaluate to TRUE at that time. *Contrast* relvar constraint (second definition); this latter is a formal construct, but relvar predicates are necessarily somewhat informal. *Note*: Relvar predicates are sometimes called business rules, q.v.—though some writers take this latter term to include a variety of other constructs in addition to relvar predicates as such, including in particular the informal counterparts to various integrity constraints. (Conversely, others regard these additional constructs as part of the relvar predicates. There's no consensus on such matters.)

Example: The relvar predicate for relvar S is "Supplier S# is under contract, is named SNAME, has status STATUS, and is located in CITY." At least, this predicate is the one assumed (and indeed stated) elsewhere in this dictionary to be the one for relvar S. However, it would be more accurate to say the predicate is, rather, "We *know* that—or (perhaps better) we *believe* that—supplier S# is under contract, is named SNAME, has status STATUS, and is located in CITY." The point is, there can't be any guarantee that the database truly reflects the state of affairs that exists in the real world (*see* correctness); all it can do is reflect what users tell it, and what users tell it in turn will reflect their beliefs about the real world, not necessarily the real world per se. But it's customary to ignore such considerations in informal contexts.

relvar reference Syntactically, a relvar name, used to denote either the relvar as such or the value of that relvar, as the context demands.

REMOVE *See* **A.**

renaming Let *r* be a relation, let *A* be an attribute of *r,* and let *r* not have an attribute named *B.* Then the renaming *r* RENAME (*A* AS *B*) is a relation with (a) heading identical to that of *r* except that attribute *A* in that heading is renamed *B,* and (b) body identical to that of *r* except that all references to *A* in that body (more precisely, in tuples in that body) are replaced by references to *B. See also* tuple renaming.

Example: The expression

```
  P RENAME ( WEIGHT AS WT )
```

yields a relation identical to the current value of relvar P, except that attribute WEIGHT is renamed WT. Note that relvar P per se remains unaltered in the database—RENAME is not like ALTER TABLE in SQL, it's just a read-only operator that (like restrict, for example) takes a certain relation as input and returns another as output. *Note*: For reasons of user friendliness, **Tutorial D** allows two or more consecutive renamings to be expressed by means of a single RENAME invocation. Thus, for example, the expression (P RENAME (WEIGHT AS WT)) RENAME (COLOR AS COL) can be abbreviated to P RENAME (WEIGHT AS WT, COLOR AS COL). A similar remark applies to several other relational (and tuple) operations also—for example, EXTEND, SUMMARIZE, and so on.

repeating group Let some table have a column C of type T. Then C is a repeating group column if and only if the values appearing within C aren't values of type T but are, rather, collections (sets or lists or arrays or . . .) of values of type T. Repeating groups are outlawed in the relational model (which is why this definition is phrased in terms of tables and columns instead of relations and attributes); in fact, a "relation" with a repeating group "attribute" is a contradiction in terms.

restriction Let r be a relation and let bx be a restriction condition, q.v., on r (observe in particular, therefore, that every attribute reference in bx identifies some attribute of r). Then the restriction of r according to bx, r WHERE bx, is a relation with heading the same as that of r and body consisting of all tuples of r for which bx evaluates to TRUE.
Note: Restriction is sometimes known as selection, but it shouldn't be confused with the SELECT operation of SQL. The SQL SELECT operation—meaning, more specifically, just the SELECT portion of an SQL SELECT expression, q.v.—can be loosely characterized as a combination of summarize, extend, rename, and "project" ("project" in quotes because it doesn't eliminate duplicates, in general, unless explicitly requested to do so via DISTINCT).

Example: The following expression denotes a restriction of the relation that's the current value of relvar P:

```
P WHERE WEIGHT < WEIGHT ( 17.5 )
```

restriction condition A Boolean expression in which (a) all attribute references identify attributes of the same relation *r* and (b) there are no relvar references. *See* restriction. *Note*: WHERE clauses in real languages usually permit predicates that are considerably more general than simple restriction conditions on the pertinent relation. Strictly speaking, in fact, a restriction condition isn't even allowed to contain any connectives, since the connectives are logical operators, not algebraic ones. In practice, however, the following identities let real languages support the connectives after all:

```
r WHERE ( p AND q )
       ≡ ( r WHERE p ) INTERSECT ( r WHERE q )

r WHERE ( p OR q )
       ≡ ( r WHERE p ) UNION ( r WHERE q )

r WHERE ( NOT p )
       ≡ r MINUS ( r WHERE p )
```

Examples: For an example of a WHERE clause in which the predicate is just a simple restriction condition on the pertinent relation, see restriction. Here by contrast is an example in which the predicate is more general:

```
S WHERE P { P# } =
( ( SP RENAME ( S# AS SNO ) ) WHERE SNO = S# ) { P# }
```

The predicate here isn't just a simple restriction condition on the relation that's the current value of relvar S, because (a) it contains attribute references that don't identify attributes of that relation, and (b) it also contains two relvar references (to P and SP, respectively). However, the overall expression can be seen as shorthand for something like the following:

```
WITH ( SP RENAME ( S# AS SNO ) ) AS t1 ,
     ( EXTEND S ADD ( ( P { P# } ) AS X ) ) AS t2 ,
     ( EXTEND t2 ADD
     ( ( ( t1 WHERE SNO = S# ) { P# } ) AS Y ) )
                                          AS t3 :
  t3 WHERE X = Y
```

In this expanded formulation, X and Y are (relation valued) attributes of *t3*, and the predicate in the WHERE clause in the last line is indeed a restriction condition as formally defined.

reversible decomposition Replacing a relvar *R* by a set of relvars *R1, R2, . . ., Rn* in such a way that it's guaranteed that *R* can be derived from *R1, R2, . . ., Rn*. Nonloss decomposition, q.v., is an important special case.

rewrite rule An identity, q.v., in the sense of the fourth definition of that term. As the name suggests, a rewrite rule of the form $x = y$ allows any expression that contains an occurrence of x to be rewritten as an expression that contains an occurrence of y instead. *See* expression transformation; query rewrite; substitution.

right associativity *See* left associativity.

ring (mathematics) A formal system that obeys all of The Laws of Algebra, q.v., except that the commutative, identity, and inverse laws don't necessarily apply to multiplication. *Note*: Every ring is a commutative group, q.v., with respect to addition.

RM/T An extended form of the relational model, due to Codd, with the explicit goal of capturing more meaning than the relational model per se is capable of. The name is an abbreviation for Relational Model / Tasmania (so called because Codd first described it at a conference in Tasmania). RM/T includes a variety of "semantic" constructs (e.g., E- and P-relations, which are meant to represent entities and properties, respectively, together with operators for operating on such relations). RM/T has never been implemented in a commercial product (in fact it couldn't be, since the sole formal paper on the topic—"Extending the Database Relational Model to

Capture More Meaning," *ACM TODS 4,* No. 4—fails to specify it adequately), but its ideas can be useful as an aid in conventional database design.

RM/V1 *See* RM/V2.

RM/V2 Codd spent much of the late 1980s revising and extending the original relational model, which he referred to as "the Relational Model Version 1" or RM/V1, to produce "the Relational Model Version 2" or RM/V2. As noted in the introduction to this dictionary, however, definitions herein are intended to conform to the relational model as defined by *The Third Manifesto*; in consequence, they don't always agree with Codd's RM/V1 or RM/V2 definitions. For details of these latter, see Codd's book *The Relational Model for Database Management Version 2* (Addison-Wesley, 1990).

row 1. SQL analog of either a tuple value or a tuple variable, as the context demands. 2. More generally, a picture of a tuple (on paper, for example). *See also* cell; column; table.

row ID An implementation construct (typically though not necessarily some kind of pointer, q.v.). In some commercial products, however, such IDs are exposed to the user—usually, and unfortunately, in such a way as to violate either The Information Principle or The Principle of Interchangeability or both. Sometimes rather inappropriately called a tuple ID.

rule of inference *See* inference rule.

RVA Relation valued attribute.

S

safe expression An expression that would be guaranteed to evaluate to a finite result even if the underlying domains were infinite. In practice, various rules are imposed to ensure that unsafe expressions can never occur. An example of an unsafe expression, if it were permitted, would be one denoting the set of all supplier tuples not currently appearing in relvar S (in other words, a request for the complement of the relation that's the current value of relvar S). *Note*: As should be obvious, it's generally desirable to prohibit unsafe expressions even if all domains are in fact finite (as of course they are in real systems).

scalar 1. (*Of a type, attribute, value, or variable*) Having no user-visible component parts. The term is also often used as an abbreviation for *scalar value* specifically. 2. (*Of an operator*) Returning a scalar result. *Note*: Scalar types, attributes, and values are required by the relational model; scalar variables aren't, but they're almost certainly needed in the external environment in order to support, e.g., retrieval of the value of some scalar attribute from some tuple of some relation. Similar remarks apply to scalar operators. Note too that there's no such thing as "absolute scalarness" (or "absolute atomicity," as it's sometimes called)—the concept is necessarily somewhat relative. For example, a phone number might be perceived equally well as an "atomic" (i.e., scalar) value or as a tuple value consisting of country code, area code, and local number (and a database design involving phone numbers ought to be capable of supporting both perceptions). Consider also the case of TABLE_DUM, which is clearly a relation and yet (like a scalar) has no user-visible component parts.

scalar attribute *See* scalar.

scalar type *See* scalar.

scalar value *See* scalar.

scalar variable *See* scalar.

Second Great Blunder, The Mixing pointers and relations. *See* pointer. Note that committing The First Great Blunder, q.v., seems to lead inevitably to committing the second as well; however, it's possible to commit the second without committing the first.

second normal form Relvar R is in second normal form, 2NF, if and only if every nonkey attribute A of R is such that the set $\{A\}$ is irreducibly dependent on every key of R; equivalently, if and only if, for every nontrivial FD $A \rightarrow B$, satisfied by R (a) A is either a superkey or not a subkey or (b) B is a subkey. Every 2NF relvar is in 1NF (as is every relvar, in fact). *Note*: Although being in 2NF clearly doesn't preclude being in the next higher normal form (3NF) as well, the term *2NF* is often used loosely to refer to a relvar that's in 2NF and not in 3NF. Also, second normal form as such is no longer very important (BCNF, 5NF, and 6NF being the normal forms of most practical significance); we mention it here mainly for historical reasons.

Example: As noted under Boyce/Codd normal form, with the normal forms it's often more instructive to show a counterexample rather than an example per se. Suppose for the sake of the example, therefore, that relvar SP has an additional attribute CITY, representing the city of the applicable supplier. This revised version of SP satisfies the FD $\{S\#\} \rightarrow \{CITY\}$, and is therefore not in 2NF (because CITY is a nonkey attribute, yet $\{CITY\}$ isn't irreducibly dependent on the key $\{S\#,P\#\}$; equivalently, $\{S\#\}$ isn't a superkey, *is* a subkey, and $\{CITY\}$ isn't a subkey).

second order logic A form of predicate logic in which the sets over which variables range are allowed to contain predicates. *Contrast* first order logic.

Example: Consider the well known principle of mathematical induction, limited here for simplicity to its application to monadic predicates p whose sole parameter is of type nonnegative integer. That principle can be stated (in somewhat stilted English) as follows: For all such predicates p, if (a) $p(0)$ is true and (b) for all i, if $p(i)$ is true then $p(i+1)$ is true, then (c) $p(n)$ is true for all n. In symbols:

```
FORALL p ( ( p(0) AND
                  FORALL i ( p(i) IMPLIES p(i+1) ) )
        IMPLIES FORALL n ( p(n) ) )
```

In this example the variables i and n range over nonnegative integers, but the variable p ranges over predicates (specifically, monadic predicates whose sole parameter is of type nonnegative integer). The overall expression is thus second order.

SELECT expression In SQL, most queries are formulated as expressions involving, in order, a SELECT clause (with an optional DISTINCT specification), a FROM clause, a WHERE clause, a GROUP BY clause, and a HAVING clause (the last three of which are optional). Such expressions are known generically, and loosely, as SELECT - FROM - WHERE - GROUP BY - HAVING expressions, or more simply as SELECT - FROM - WHERE expressions, or more simply still as just SELECT expressions. Unfortunately, it's impossible in a dictionary of this nature to give a complete and accurate definition of this SQL construct, owing in part to the interdependencies among the various clauses; for example, the semantics of the SELECT clause depend on whether or not there's an accompanying GROUP BY clause (among other things). But the following conceptual algorithm gives a very rough idea of the overall semantics:

- (*FROM*) Form the Cartesian product of the tables specified in the FROM clause.

- (*WHERE*) Discard rows from that product that fail to satisfy the Boolean expression in the WHERE clause.

- (*GROUP BY*) Partition the rows that remain into groups in accordance with values of the columns specified in the GROUP BY clause.

- (*HAVING*) Discard groups from that partitioning that fail to satisfy the Boolean expression in the HAVING clause.

- (*SELECT*) From each group that remains, derive a row by applying whatever combination of summarize, extend, rename, and "project" operations is specified by the SELECT and GROUP BY clauses taken together.

- (*DISTINCT*) Discard redundant duplicate rows.

Here are some of the factors that would need to be taken into account in any more precise explanation:

- All of the differences listed under table between SQL tables and their relational counterparts

- The fact that the various clauses can all contain subqueries, q.v.

- The fact that certain subqueries can be "correlated"

- The fact that certain subqueries can be "lateral"

- The fact that certain fundamental operations, including equality ("=") in particular, aren't fully defined (in some cases, in fact, they're explicitly allowed to be what the SQL standard calls "possibly nondeterministic," meaning their results are unpredictable)

Further explanation of such matters is beyond the scope of this dictionary. *Note*: Let *exp1* and *exp2* be SELECT expressions. Then SQL permits various unions, intersections, and differences to be formulated in terms of *exp1* and *exp2*.

selection *See* restriction.

selector An operator—read-only by definition—for selecting, or specifying, an arbitrary value of a given type; not to be confused with the SELECT operation of SQL (for a loose characterization of this latter, *see* SELECT expression). Every type, tuple and relation types included, has at least one associated selector. *Note*: Ultimately, the only way any expression can ever yield a value of type *T* is via invocation of some selector for that type *T*. In fact, the selector notion is essentially a generalization of the familiar concept of a literal; that is, all literals are selector invocations, but some selector invocations aren't literals (to be specific, a selector invocation is a literal if and only if all of its arguments are themselves specified as literals).

Examples: Several selector invocations appear in the example under INSERT; however, those examples are all literals, since their arguments are themselves all specified as literals in turn. Here by contrast are some selector invocations that aren't literals. Let SX, PX, and QX be variables of types CHAR, CHAR, and INTEGER, respectively. Then (a) the expressions S#(SX), P#(PX), and QTY(QX) are selector invocations for types S#, P#, and QTY, respectively; (b) the expression TUPLE {S# S#(SX), P# P#(PX), QTY QTY(150)} is a selector invocation for tuple type TUPLE {S# S#, P# P#, QTY QTY}; and (c) the expression RELATION {*ts*}, where *ts* is the tuple selector invocation just shown, is a selector invocation for relation type RELATION {S# S#, P# P#, QTY QTY}. Further explanation is beyond the scope of this dictionary.

self-referencing relvar A relvar *R* with a foreign key that refers to some candidate key of *R* itself (hence giving rise to a referential cycle, q.v., of length one). Database designs involving such relvars are usually contraindicated.

semantic Pertaining to meaning or semantics (of a language, sentence, etc.). *Contrast* lexical; syntactic.

semantic modeling A rather vague term, never very precisely defined, having to do with the representation of meaning within a formal database design. Other terms used in the same or a related sense include conceptual modeling; data modeling (q.v.); entity modeling; entity/relationship modeling (q.v.); and object modeling. *See also* RM/T.

semantic optimization Using integrity constraints to help in transforming relational expressions, usually for performance purposes. *See* expression transformation; optimizer.

Example: Consider the query

```
P WHERE CITY = 'London' AND COLOR = 'Red'
```

Suppose relvar P is subject to the constraint that parts in London must be red. Then the query can clearly be transformed into the following simpler one:

```
P WHERE CITY = 'London'
```

Moreover, if the original query had requested blue parts instead of red ones, the optimizer might be able to determine that the result is empty without actually having to execute the query at all.

semantic override Same as domain check override.

semantics (*Plural word treated as singular*) Meaning; pertaining to meaning. *Note*: Semantics is often confused with syntax, especially in nontechnical contexts. But when we say something, semantics is what we mean, while syntax is merely how we say it. Semantics is more important than syntax, at least from a logical point of view.

semidifference Let *r1* and *r2* be relations. Then the semidifference between *r1* and *r2* (in that order), *r1* NOT MATCHING *r2*, is shorthand for *r1* MINUS (*r1* MATCHING *r2*).

Example: The expression

```
S NOT MATCHING SP
```

yields suppliers who currently supply no parts at all.

SEMIJOIN Same as MATCHING.

semijoin Let *r1* and *r2* be relations. Then the semijoin of *r1* with *r2* (in that order), *r1* MATCHING *r2*, is shorthand for (*r1* JOIN *r2*){*X*}, where {*X*} is the heading of *r1*. Note that *r1* MATCHING *r2* and *r2* MATCHING *r1* aren't equivalent, in general.

Example: The expression

```
S MATCHING SP
```

yields suppliers who currently supply at least one part.

SEMIMINUS Same as NOT MATCHING.

sentence *See* logical system.

SEQUEL "Structured English Query Language" (the original name for SQL).

set A collection of objects, called elements, with the property that given an arbitrary object *x,* it can be determined whether *x* appears in the collection (*see* set membership). An example is the collection {*y,x,z*}, which can equivalently be written as {*x,y,z*}, since sets have no ordering to their elements (nor do they contain any duplicate elements). Every subset of a set is itself a set. *See also* class (first definition). *Note*: There's a logical difference (actually a difference in type) between an element *x* and the set {*x*} that contains just that element *x*. Thus, a relational language needs to provide both (a) an operator for extracting the single tuple from a relation of cardinality one and (b) an operator for extracting the single attribute value from a tuple of degree one (*see* attribute extractor; tuple extractor). Note too that the inverse functionality—in effect, building up a tuple from specified attribute values and building up a relation from specified tuple values—is provided by the appropriate tuple and relation selectors (*see* selector).

set algebra *See* Boolean algebra (second definition).

set function Deprecated (because highly inappropriate) term for an aggregate operator.

set inclusion Set $s1$ includes set $s2$ ("$s1 \supseteq s2$") if and only if it is a superset of $s2$; set $s2$ is included in set $s1$ ("$s2 \subseteq s1$") if and only if it is a subset of $s1$. Set $s1$ is equal to set $s2$ ("$s1 = s2$") if and only if each includes the other. Observe that every set is included in itself, also that every set includes the empty set. Observe also that the term *set inclusion* is usually taken, a trifle arbitrarily, to refer to the "$\subseteq$" operator specifically, not the "$\supseteq$" operator. *Note*: The term *containment* is sometimes used as a synonym for inclusion in the present sense, but this usage is deprecated— better to say of a set that it *contains* its elements (*see* containment) but *includes* its subsets.

set level The operators of the relational model are all set level, in the sense that they take entire relations or relvars or both as operands and either produce entire relations as results or update entire relvars. (*Relation level* would be a better term.) *Note*: An implication of this notion for update operators in particular is that compensating actions and database integrity checking must not be done until all of the updating has been done; i.e., a set level update must not be treated as a sequence of individual tuple level updates. *Contrast* tuple level.

set membership (*Of an element*) The property of appearing in some given set; the operation of testing for that property. Set membership is usually denoted by the symbol "$\in$"; thus, for example, the Boolean expression $x \in s$ (which is semantically equivalent to the expression $\{x\} \subseteq s$) returns TRUE if and only if element x does in fact appear in set s.

set operator *See* Boolean algebra (second definition).

set theory A branch of mathematics, closely related to logic, that deals with the nature of sets; it formalizes the concept of a set in terms of certain axioms, such as the axiom of extension, q.v.

Sheffer stroke *See* NAND.

SI prefixes Part of the International System of Units, the standard for scientific measurements of all kinds (SI is an abbreviation for *Système*

Internationale d'Unités). The following table lists SI prefixes and their abbreviations and meanings:

yotta	Y	10 to the power 24	yocto	y	10 to the power -24
zetta	Z	10 to the power 21	zepto	z	10 to the power -21
exa	E	10 to the power 18	atto	a	10 to the power -18
peta	P	10 to the power 15	femto	f	10 to the power -15
tera	T	10 to the power 12	pico	p	10 to the power -12
giga	G	10 to the power 9	nano	n	10 to the power -9
mega	M	10 to the power 6	micro	µ	10 to the power -6
kilo	k	10 to the power 3	milli	m	10 to the power -3
hecto	h	10 to the power 2	centi	c	10 to the power -2
deca	da	10 to the power 1	deci	d	10 to the power -1

In the computing world, however, the prefixes yotta through kilo are used a little differently. To be specific, they're interpreted in terms of powers of 2, not 10, as indicated here:

yotta	Y	2 to the power 80
zetta	Z	2 to the power 70
exa	E	2 to the power 60
peta	P	2 to the power 50
tera	T	2 to the power 40
giga	G	2 to the power 30
mega	M	2 to the power 20
kilo	K	2 to the power 10

For example, one kilobyte (1KB—the prefix *kilo* is usually abbreviated K, not k, in the computing world) is 1,024 bytes, not 1,000 bytes. Note in particular that a gigabyte is a billion bytes, roughly speaking (the abbreviation BB is sometimes used instead of GB; likewise, the abbreviation XB is sometimes used instead of EB). Note also that—contrary to popular belief—*gigabyte* is pronounced with a soft initial *g* and the *i* is long (as in *gigantic*).

signature Let *Op* be an operator. Then the signature of *Op* consists of the combination of (a) the operator name *Op*, (b) the types (in order) of the parameters to *Op*, and (c) the type of the result, if any, of executing *Op*. *Note*: Some writers give definitions that differ slightly from the one just given; for example, the term is sometimes taken to include parameter names.

Example: Consider the read-only version of the operator DOUBLE from the examples under argument. The signature for that operator consists of the combination of (a) the operator name DOUBLE, (b) the type (INTEGER) of the sole parameter to that operator, and (c) the type (also INTEGER) of the result returned when that operator is invoked.

simple attribute An attribute, q.v. *Contrast* composite attribute.

simple key A key that's not composite.

simple predicate A predicate that involves no connectives.

simple proposition A proposition that involves no connectives.

single arrow Same as arrow (*see* functional dependency).

single-relvar constraint Term sometimes used to mean a database constraint that mentions exactly one relvar. *Contrast* multi-relvar constraint. *Note*: The difference between single-relvar and multi-relvar constraints is more a matter of pragma than logic, thanks to The Principle of Interchangeability among other things.

Examples: The key constraints for relvars S, SP, and P; also constraints C1 and C2 from the examples under database constraint.

single-tuple constraint Same as tuple constraint.

singleton Strictly, a set of cardinality one (also known as a singleton set); sometimes used loosely to refer to the single element contained in such a set.

sixth normal form Relvar R is in sixth normal form, 6NF, if and only if it can't be nonloss decomposed at all, other than trivially—i.e., if and only if the only JDs it satisfies are trivial ones. Note, therefore, that (a) 6NF is the ultimate normal form with respect to normalization as conventionally understood; (b) every 6NF relvar is in 5NF. Observe that relvar R is in 6NF if and only if (a) it consists of a key K and at most one other attribute A (if K is free of embedded dependencies, q.v.) or exactly one other attribute A (otherwise), and (b) no proper subset $\{B\}$ of K satisfies either the FD $\{A\} \rightarrow \{B\}$ or the FD $\{B\} \rightarrow \{A\}$. Observe also that the definition can in fact be simplified thus: Relvar R is in 6NF if and only if it's in 5NF, is of degree n, and has no key of degree less than $n-1$. *Note*: The concept of 6NF is given an extended definition in a temporal database context, where it enjoys certain advantages over 5NF—advantages that don't necessarily apply in a conventional (nontemporal) database. The details are beyond the scope of this dictionary.

Examples: 1. Relvar SP is in 6NF, since it can't be nonloss decomposed at all other than trivially. (Observe that SP is certainly in 5NF; it's of degree three; and it has no key of degree less than two.) By contrast, relvars S and P aren't in 6NF, because they can both be nonloss decomposed, nontrivially, into several binary projections. 2. Let relvar PLUS have attributes A, B, and C, all of type INTEGER, and let the corresponding relvar predicate be $A + B = C$. Then relvar PLUS has three distinct keys: {A,B}, {B,C}, and {C,A}. But PLUS is in 6NF, since it's certainly in 5NF, it's of degree three, and it has no key of degree less than two.

Skolem constant By definition, the expression EXISTS x $(p(x))$ is logically equivalent to the expression $p(v)$ for some unknown value v; that is, the original expression asserts that some such v certainly exists, even if we don't know what it is. That value v is a Skolem constant. *See also* Skolem function.

Skolem function By definition, the expression FORALL y (EXISTS x $(q(y,x))$ is logically equivalent to the expression FORALL y $(q(y,f(y)))$ for some unknown function f of the universally quantified variable y. That function f is a Skolem function. Together, Skolem constants, q.v., and Skolem functions provide a basis for systematically eliminating existential quantifiers from an arbitrary expression, thereby making that expression more amenable to subsequent formal manipulation. Further details are beyond the scope of this dictionary.

Small Divide One of the many relational division operators that have been defined over the years (*see* division). Let relations *r1, r2,* and *r3* be such that (a) attributes with the same name in *r1* and *r3* are of the same type, and so are attributes with the same name in *r3* and *r2* (in other words, *r1* and *r3* are joinable, and so are *r3* and *r2*); (b) the set $\{X\}$ is the common attributes of *r1* and *r3*; (c) the set $\{Y\}$ is the common attributes of *r3* and *r2*; and (d) the sets $\{X\}$ and $\{Y\}$ are disjoint. Then the division *r1* DIVIDEBY *r2* PER (*r3*)—where *r1* is the dividend, *r2* is the divisor, and *r3* is the "mediator"—is a relation with the same heading as *r1* and with body defined as follows: tuple *t* appears in that body if and only if it appears in *r1* and a tuple <*x,y*> with *x* equal to the *X* value in *t* appears in *r3*$\{X,Y\}$ for all tuples <*y*> in *r2*$\{Y\}$. In other words, the expression *r1* DIVIDEBY *r2* PER (*r3*) is semantically equivalent to the expression *r1* NOT MATCHING ((*r1*$\{X\}$ JOIN *r2*$\{Y\}$) NOT MATCHING *r3*). *Contrast* Great Divide.

Example: The division S DIVIDEBY P PER (SP) yields a relation with heading the same as that of relvar S and body consisting of all possible tuples <*s#,sn,st,sc*> from relvar S such that supplier *s#* supplies all parts mentioned in relvar P. (Given the sample values of Figure 1, the result contains just the tuple for supplier S1.) The expression is semantically equivalent to this one:

```
S NOT MATCHING
    ( ( S { S# } JOIN P { P# } ) NOT MATCHING SP )
```

An equivalent tuple calculus formulation is:

```
SX   RANGES OVER { S }  ;
SPX  RANGES OVER { SP } ;
PX   RANGES OVER { P }  ;

SX WHERE FORALL PX ( EXISTS SPX
          ( SPX.S# = SX.S# AND SPX.P# = PX.P# ) )
```

An equivalent **Tutorial D** formulation is:

```
S WHERE ( !!SP ) { P# } = P { P# }
```

(*see* image relation).

snapshot A derived relvar that's real, not virtual (*contrast* view). The value of a given snapshot at a given time is the result of evaluating a certain relational expression (the snapshot defining expression, specified when the snapshot per se is defined) at some time prior to the time in question. The snapshot is "refreshed" (meaning the snapshot defining expression is reevaluated and the result assigned as the new current value of the snapshot) on demand or, more usually, when some prescribed event occurs, such as the passing of a certain interval of time.
Note: The snapshot defining expression must mention at least one relvar, for otherwise the snapshot wouldn't be, specifically, a relation variable.

Example: The following statement defines a snapshot called LSS:

```
VAR LSS SNAPSHOT ( S WHERE CITY = 'London' )
          REFRESH EVERY DAY ;
```

The relation that's the value of snapshot LSS at any given time is equal to the value of the snapshot defining expression S WHERE CITY = 'London' as it was at most 24 hours prior to the time in question.

sort/merge A join implementation technique.

sorted logic A form of logic in which the values that are the subject of the logic are divided into *sorts* (i.e., types). *Note:* Most logic texts pay little or no attention to the notion of types; instead, they deal with unsorted logic, which effectively means they assume that everything is of the same type (often referred to as "the universe of discourse").

soundness That property of a formal system according to which, given a set *s* of sentences of the system, no sentence not implied by those in *s* can be derived using the rules of inference of that system (i.e., all theorems are tautologies). *Contrast* completeness.

source relvar For the general meaning, *see* inclusion dependency. In the foreign key context in particular, the term is sometimes used as a synonym for referencing relvar, q.v.

source tuple Term sometimes used in the foreign key context as a synonym for referencing tuple, q.v.

SQL The best known attempt (unfortunately a seriously flawed one) to realize the abstract ideas of the relational model in concrete syntactic form. The name SQL—the official pronunciation is "ess cue ell," though it's often pronounced "sequel" (*see* SEQUEL)—was originally an abbreviation for *Structured Query Language*. In its standard incarnation, however, the name is just a name and isn't considered to be an abbreviation for anything at all. The version of the SQL standard current at the time of writing is SQL:2003 (so called because it was ratified in 2003); the next and probably (?) final version is likely to be ratified in 2008.

star join A join implementation technique.

state constraint A database constraint that isn't a transition constraint.

statement 1. (*Logic*) A proposition. 2. (*Programming languages*) A construct that causes some action to occur, such as defining or updating a variable or changing the flow of control. *Contrast* expression. *Note:* Throughout this dictionary, the term *statement* should be understood in the programming language sense, unless the context demands otherwise.

Example (*second definition only*): See the examples under expression.

stored procedure A subroutine, possibly parameterized; in other words, an operator. *Note*: Like the term *encapsulated,* q.v., the term *stored procedure* has come to mean something that unfortunately mixes model and implementation considerations. From the point of view of the model, a stored procedure is indeed, as just stated, nothing more than an operator. In practice, however, stored procedures have a number of properties that make them much more important than they would be if they were just operators as such (although the first two of the following properties will probably apply to operators in general, at least if the operators in question are system defined). First, they're compiled separately and can be shared by distinct applications. Second, their compiled code is, typically, physically stored at the site at which the data itself is physically stored, with obvious performance benefits. Third, they're often used to provide shared functionality that ought to have been provided by the DBMS but isn't (integrity checking is a good example here). *See also* triggered procedure.

subexpression An expression nested inside another such.

subject to update Let *Op* be an update operator that, when invoked, updates the argument corresponding to parameter *x*. Then parameter *x* is said to be subject to update (and any argument corresponding to *x* must be a variable specifically).

Example: See the second example under argument.

subkey Loosely, a subset of a key. More precisely, let X be a subset of the heading of relvar R; then X is a subkey for R if and only if there exists some key K for R such that K is a superset of X.

Examples: The subkeys for relvar SP are {S#,P#}, {S#}, {P#}, and {}. Note that the empty set {} is necessarily a subkey for all possible relvars R.

subquery In general, a relational expression nested inside another such; in SQL, a SELECT expression in parentheses.

subset Set $s2$ is a subset of set $s1$ ("$s2 \subseteq s1$") if and only if every element of $s2$ is also an element of $s1$. Observe that every set is a subset of itself, also that the empty set is a subset of every set. *Contrast* proper subset.

substitution 1. (*Logic*) Let $x1$ be an expression containing an occurrence of $y1$ as a subexpression; let $y2$ be equivalent to $y1$; and let $x2$ be the expression obtained by substituting $y2$ for the occurrence of $y1$ in question in $x1$. Then $x1$ and $x2$ are logically equivalent. 2. (*View implementation*) A technique for implementing operations on views, according to which references to view V are replaced by the view defining expression for V (*contrast* view materialization). 3. (*Operator invocation*) Replacing a parameter by an argument. 4. ("*What if*") In **Tutorial D**, the name *substitute* is used to refer to the "what if" operator, q.v.

Examples: 1. (*Logic*) *See* the example under expression transformation. 2. (*View implementation*) *See* the second example under pseudovariable reference.

subtables and supertables A scheme according to which some table $T2$ is specified to have all of the columns of some other table $T1$ together with certain additional columns of its own (*see* table). One of the numerous reasons for deprecating any such scheme is that which of $T1$ and $T2$ is regarded as the subtable and which the supertable can depend on the system in question.

subtuple A subset of a tuple; hence, a tuple.

subtype *See* type inheritance.

summarization Let relations *r1* and *r2* be such that *r2* is of the same type as some projection of *r1*, and let the attributes of *r2* be *A1, A2, . . ., An*. Then the summarization SUMMARIZE *r1* PER (*r2*) ADD (*exp* AS *X*) is a relation with (a) heading the heading of *r2* extended with attribute *X*, and (b) body consisting of all tuples *t* such that *t* is a tuple of *r2* extended with a value *x* for attribute *X*. That value *x* is computed by evaluating the expression *exp* over all tuples of *r1* that have the same value for attributes *A1, A2, . . ., An* as tuple *t* does. Relation *r2* must not have an attribute called *X*, and *exp* must not refer to *X*. *Note*: The expression *exp* will normally include at least one summary, q.v. Also, earlier versions of **Tutorial D** supported the SUMMARIZE operator explicitly; by contrast, the current version provides equivalent functionality as part of its support for the EXTEND operator, q.v. The examples that follow illustrate both styles.

Examples: The following expression denotes a summarization of the relation that's the current value of relvar SP:

```
SUMMARIZE SP PER ( S { S# } ) ADD ( COUNT ( ) AS CT )
```

That summarization is a relation of type RELATION {S# S#, CT INTEGER}, containing one tuple for each distinct S# value currently appearing in relvar S (not SP!—note the PER specification), and no other tuples. Each such tuple contains a supplier number and a count of the number of times that supplier number currently appears in relvar SP (the expression COUNT() is an example of a summary, q.v.). Given the sample values in Figure 1, for example, the tuple for supplier S2 in the result has S# value S2 and CT value two, and the tuple for supplier S5 has S# value S5 and CT value zero. By contrast, the expression

```
SUMMARIZE SP PER ( SP { S# } ) ADD ( COUNT ( ) AS CT )
```

—which (because the PER operand is a projection of the SUMMARIZE operand) can in fact be simplified, slightly, to

```
SUMMARIZE SP BY { S# } ADD ( COUNT ( ) AS CT )
```
—yields a relation of type RELATION {S# S#, CT INTEGER} with one tuple for each distinct S# value currently appearing in relvar SP. Given the sample values in Figure 1, for example, the result contains no tuple for supplier S5.

Here now are analogs of the foregoing examples that make use of EXTEND instead of SUMMARIZE:

```
EXTEND S { S# } ADD ( COUNT ( !!SP ) AS CT )

EXTEND SP { S# } ADD ( COUNT ( !!SP ) AS CT )
```

The expression !!SP in these examples is shorthand for the expression (SP MATCHING RELATION {TUPLE {S# S#}}){ALL BUT S#}. For further explanation, *see* image relation.

SUMMARIZE *See* summarization.

summary A construct that can appear within the ADD specification within a SUMMARIZE expression (*see* summarization). Note that summaries aren't aggregate operator invocations, though they might look rather like them. An aggregate operator invocation is an expression, and it can appear wherever a literal of the appropriate type can appear. A summary, by contrast, is merely an operand to SUMMARIZE (speaking a trifle loosely); it isn't an expression, it has no meaning outside the context of SUMMARIZE, and in fact can't appear outside that context.

superkey Loosely, a superset of a key; it has the uniqueness property but not necessarily the irreducibility property. More precisely, let X be a subset of the heading of relvar R; then X is a superkey for R if and only if no possible value for R contains two distinct tuples with the same value for X.

Examples: Relvar S has exactly eight superkeys (why?), of which {S#} and {S#,CITY} are two. Note that the heading of any given relvar R is necessarily a superkey for R.

superset Set $s1$ is a superset of set $s2$ ("$s1 \supseteq s2$") if and only if every element of $s2$ is also an element of $s1$. Observe that every set is a superset of itself, also that every set is a superset of the empty set. *Contrast* proper superset.

supertype *See* type inheritance.

surjection A mapping, or function, from set $s1$ to set $s2$ such that each element of $s2$ is the image of at least one element of $s1$ (in other words, a many-to-one correspondence, in the strict sense of that term). Also known as a surjective or "many-to-one onto" mapping.

Example: Let $s1$ and $s2$ be the set of all integers and the set of all nonnegative integers, respectively. Then the mapping from integers x to their absolute values $|x|$ is a surjection from $s1$ to $s2$.

surrogate Abbreviation for surrogate key.

surrogate key A single-attribute key with the property that its values serve solely as surrogates—hence the name—for the entities they're supposed to stand for (in other words, they serve merely to represent the fact that the corresponding entities exist, and they carry absolutely no additional information or meaning). *Contrast* composite key; intelligent key.

symmetric difference (set theory) The set of all elements appearing in either but not both of two given sets. *Note*: Symmetric difference is to exclusive OR as union is to inclusive OR.

symmetry 1. (*Of a dyadic logical operator*) Commutativity. 2. (*Of a binary relation*) The binary relation r is symmetric if and only if, for all x and y, if the tuple $<x,y>$ appears in r, then so does the tuple $<y,x>$.

Examples (*first definition only*): The logical operator EQUIV; the equality operator "=".

syntactic Pertaining to grammatical structure or syntax (of a language, sentence, etc.). *Contrast* lexical; semantic.

syntax *See* semantics.

system defined *See* user defined.

T

table 1. SQL analog of either a relation or a relvar, as the context demands. Here are some of the major differences between tables in SQL and their relational counterparts: (a) SQL tables can contain duplicate rows; (b) SQL tables can contain nulls; (c) SQL tables have a left-to-right column sequence; (d) SQL tables can have two or more columns with the same name; (e) SQL tables can have what are, in effect, columns with no name at all. 2. More generally, a picture of a relation (on paper, for example). *Note*: Confusion between relations and such tabular pictures probably accounts for the popular misconception that relations are "flat" or two-dimensional. While it's obviously true that those pictures are two-dimensional, relations in general aren't; rather, a relation of degree n is n-dimensional, in the sense that its tuples correspond to points in some n-dimensional space (one dimension for each attribute of the relation in question). One specific consequence of such considerations is that (again contrary to popular opinion) relations are perfectly capable of representing so called multidimensional data and thereby supporting so called online analytical processing (OLAP). *See also* cell; column; row.

table alias *See* alias.

TABLE_DEE and TABLE_DUM Two relation constants, preferably built in. TABLE_DEE is the unique relation with no attributes and exactly one tuple (necessarily the empty tuple); TABLE_DUM is the unique relation with no attributes and no tuples at all. They can be interpreted as TRUE (or *yes*) and FALSE (or *no*), respectively. (More precisely, the relation predicate for TABLE_DEE is any 0-place predicate that evaluates to TRUE, and the relation predicate for TABLE_DUM is any 0-place predicate that evaluates to FALSE.) *Note*: The names are perhaps not very well chosen, since TABLE_DEE and TABLE_DUM are precisely the two relations that are most difficult to picture as tables.

tables and views / tables or views Phrases that often appear in SQL contexts and strongly suggest that views are somehow different from tables. But the whole point about views is that (in SQL terms) they *are* tables—just as, in mathematics, the whole point about a set that's (e.g.) the union or intersection of two sets is that it is itself a set. Views should "look and feel" just like base tables to the user (The Principle of Interchangeability translated into SQL terms).

target key *See* foreign key.

target relvar 1. (*In an IND*) For the general meaning, *see* inclusion dependency. In the foreign key context in particular, the term is sometimes used as a synonym for referenced relvar, q.v. 2. (*In an assignment*) The relvar being updated in a relational assignment operation.

target tuple Term sometimes used in the foreign key context as a synonym for referenced tuple, q.v.

tautology A predicate whose every possible invocation is guaranteed to yield TRUE, regardless of what arguments are substituted for its parameters. *Contrast* contradiction.

Examples: Let $p1$ be the predicate (actually a proposition) $2+2 = 4$; let $p2$ be the predicate $x = x$, where x denotes an arbitrary integer; and let $p3$ be the predicate (p) OR $(NOT(p))$, where p denotes an arbitrary proposition. Then $p1$, $p2$, and $p3$ are all tautologies.

TCLOSE *See* transitive closure.

temporal database A database in which at least one of the relvars is temporal (where a temporal relvar is one whose heading includes at least one attribute of some timestamp type, implying that the corresponding relvar predicate has at least one parameter of some timestamp type). A variety of special operators can be defined to help with the management of such databases—see the book *Temporal Data and the Relational Model*, by C. J. Date, Hugh Darwen, and Nikos A. Lorentzos (Morgan Kaufmann, 2003)—but all of those operators are, in the final analysis, shorthand for something that can already be expressed in the classical relational algebra. Further details are beyond the scope of this dictionary.

theorem Something that follows from given axioms according to given rules of inference (and is therefore true if the axioms are true and the inference rules valid). In the database context, tuples in derived relations can be regarded as theorems, because they represent propositions derived from the ones represented by tuples in the base relations. Theorems include axioms, q.v., as a degenerate special case. *See* proof.

Example: Given the sample values of Figure 1, the relation denoted by the expression (S JOIN P){S#,P#} contains the tuple <S1,P1>. That tuple can be regarded as a theorem; it represents the (true) proposition "Supplier S1 and part P1 are in the same city," a fact that can be inferred from the axioms represented by tuples in the base relations.

theta join A relational operation, equivalent to an expression of the form (*r1* TIMES *r2*) WHERE *A1 theta A2,* where (a) *A1* and *A2* are attributes (of the same type *T*) of *r1* and *r2,* respectively, and (b) *theta* is any comparison operator that makes sense for values of type *T* (e.g., "=", ">").

Example: The following expression represents the greater-than join (i.e., theta here is ">") of suppliers and parts, in that order, on cities:

```
( ( S RENAME ( CITY AS SC ) ) TIMES
  ( P RENAME ( CITY AS PC ) ) ) WHERE SC > PC
```

We assume here that CHAR—the type of attribute CITY—is an ordinal type (">" on CHAR values presumably means "greater in alphabetic ordering"). Note that we could replace TIMES by JOIN in the foregoing expression without changing the meaning. Also, replacing ">" with "<" would yield a less-than join; replacing it with "=" would yield an equijoin.

Third Manifesto, The A formal proposal for the future of data and database management systems; like Codd's original papers, it can be seen as an abstract blueprint for the design of a DBMS and the language interface to such a DBMS. *See* the introduction to this dictionary.

third normal form Relvar *R* is in third normal form, 3NF, if and only if, for every nontrivial FD $A \rightarrow B$ satisfied by *R*, *A* is a superkey or *B* is a subkey. Every 3NF relvar is in 2NF. *Note*: Many of the definitions of "3NF" in the literature are actually definitions of BCNF; *caveat lector*. Also, although being in 3NF clearly doesn't preclude being in the next higher normal form (BCNF) as well, the term *3NF* is often used loosely to refer to a relvar that's in 3NF and not in BCNF. In any case, third normal form as such is no longer very important (BCNF, 5NF, and 6NF being the normal forms of most practical significance); we mention it here mainly for historical reasons.

Example: As noted under Boyce/Codd normal form, with the normal forms it's often more instructive to show a counterexample rather than an example per se. Suppose, therefore, that relvar S satisfies the additional FD {CITY} → {STATUS}; that is, the status for a given supplier is a function of that supplier's location. Since {CITY} isn't a superkey and {STATUS} isn't a subkey, this version of relvar S isn't in 3NF (though it is in 2NF).

three-valued logic A logic in which there's a "third truth value," usually called UNKNOWN, in addition to the usual TRUE and FALSE; abbreviated 3VL. SQL is loosely based on such a logic (the relational model, by contrast, is based on two-valued logic, q.v.). In particular, SQL's support for nulls, q.v., is based on a three-valued logic, though in fact that support is logically flawed; for example, SQL treats UNKNOWN and null as identical, even though there's a logical difference between the two—UNKNOWN is a value, while null isn't a value at all but a "mark." (This is just one of many logical errors in SQL's 3VL support.) *Note*: Tautologies in 2VL aren't necessarily tautologies in 3VL; likewise, contradictions in 2VL aren't necessarily contradictions in 3VL. As a result, theorems that hold in 2VL don't necessarily hold in 3VL, and expression transformations that are valid in 2VL aren't necessarily valid in 3VL.

time-varying relation Codd's original term for a relvar; the term is deprecated because relations are values and so don't vary over time.

TIMES *See* Cartesian product.

total database constraint *See* database constraint.

total function A partial function in which every element x of the domain has an image y in the codomain; in other words, a function.

total ordering A special case of partial ordering, q.v. Let s be a set. Then a total ordering on s is a partial ordering, usually denoted "<", with the property that for all pairs of distinct elements x and y in s, either $x < y$ or $y < x$ (and not both). *Note:* Given that the "=" operator and the NOT connective are both always available, it follows that all of the usual comparison operators—"=", "≠", "<", "≤", ">", and "≥"—are available for all pairs of values in such a set s.

Examples: See the examples under ordinal type.

total relvar constraint *See* relvar constraint.

transaction A unit of recovery and concurrency; loosely, a unit of work. Transactions are all or nothing, in the sense that they either execute in their entirety or have no effect. *Note:* Transactions are often said to be a unit of integrity also. Since the relational model requires all integrity checking to be immediate, however, the unit of integrity as far as the relational model is concerned is the statement, not the transaction. *See* atomic statement; immediate checking.

transition constraint A database constraint that limits the transitions a given database can validly make from one state to another. *Contrast* state constraint.

Example ("No supplier's status must ever decrease"):

```
CONSTRAINT TRC1 IS_EMPTY (
  ( ( S' { S#, STATUS } RENAME ( STATUS AS STATUS' ) )
    JOIN
    ( S { S#, STATUS } ) )
  WHERE STATUS' > STATUS ) ;
```

This formulation relies on a convention to the effect that a primed relvar name such as S' refers to the corresponding relvar as it was prior to the update under consideration.

transitive closure Let r be a binary relation with attributes A and B, both of type T. Then the transitive closure of r, TCLOSE (r), is a relation r^+ defined as follows: the tuple $<a,b>$ appears in r^+ if and only if it appears in r or there exists a value c of type T such that the tuple $<a,c>$ appears in r and the tuple $<c,b>$ appears in r^+. (Note that this is a recursive definition; note too that r^+ is indeed a transitive relation, as the name "transitive closure" suggests. *See* transitivity, second definition.) As the following pseudocode algorithm indicates, computing TCLOSE (r) conceptually involves iterative formation of the union of some intermediate result (computed on the previous iteration) and a new partial result (computed on the current iteration), until that union ceases to grow—in other words, until it reaches a fixed point or "fixpoint."

```
r⁺ := r ;
do until r⁺ ceases to grow ;
    r⁺ := WITH ( r⁺ RENAME ( B AS C ) ) AS t1 ,
               ( r RENAME ( A AS C ) ) AS t2 :
         r⁺ UNION ( ( t1 JOIN t2 ) { A, B } ) ;
end do ;
```

See also recursive query.

transitive FD The FDs $A \rightarrow B$ and $B \rightarrow C$ together imply the transitive FD $A \rightarrow C$. (Thus, if relvar R satisfy the FDs $A \rightarrow B$ and $B \rightarrow C$, it also satisfies the transitive FD $A \rightarrow C$.)

transitivity 1. (*Of a dyadic logical operator*) The dyadic logical operator *Op*, which we assume for definiteness is expressed in infix style, is transitive if and only if, for all x, y, and z, if x *Op* y and y *Op* z are both true, then so is x *Op* z. 2. (*Of a binary relation*) The binary relation r is transitive if and only if, for all x, y, and z, if the tuples $<x,y>$ and $<y,z>$ both appear in r, then so does the tuple $<x,z>$. 3. (*Of FDs*) *See* Armstrong's inference rules.

Examples (*first definition only*): The logical operator IMPLIES; the "less than" operator "<".

TransRelational^TM **Model** A proprietary DBMS implementation technology, not based on conventional direct image techniques.

TRC Tuple relational calculus.

trigger *See* triggered procedure.

triggered procedure Strictly, an action (the "triggered action") to be performed if a specified event (the "triggering event") occurs, though the term is often used loosely to include the triggering event as well. A triggered procedure can be thought of as a stored procedure (q.v.), except that stored procedures must be explicitly invoked, whereas a triggered procedure is invoked automatically whenever the triggering event occurs. Apart from this difference, however, triggered procedures have many of the same properties, and are used for many of the same purposes, as stored procedures. No triggered procedures are prescribed by the relational model, but they aren't necessarily proscribed either—though they would be if they could lead to a violation of The Assignment Principle, q.v., which they very well might in practice. Foreign key rules provide a pragmatically important example (in which, as it happens, the "procedure" is specified declaratively). *Note*: The combination of a triggering event and the corresponding triggered action is often known simply as a trigger.

trivial decomposition A nonloss decomposition, q.v., that's performed on the basis of some trivial dependency (i.e., a trivial FD, JD, or MVD, q.v.).

Examples: 1. The suppliers relvar S can be trivially decomposed into its projections on {S#,SNAME} and {S#,SNAME,STATUS,CITY}. 2. Any relvar can be trivially decomposed into just its identity projection.

trivial FD An FD that can't possibly be violated. The FD $A \rightarrow B$ is trivial if and only if A is a superset of B.

trivial JD A JD that can't possibly be violated. The JD $\bowtie \{A1,A2,...,An\}$ is trivial if and only if at least one of $A1$, $A2$, . . ., An is the entire heading of the pertinent relvar R.

trivial MVD An MVD that can't possibly be violated. The MVD $A \rightarrow\rightarrow B$ is trivial if and only if either A is a superset of B or the set theory union of A and B is the heading of the pertinent relvar R (or both).

TRUE *See* BOOLEAN.

truth functional completeness A logical system is truth functionally complete if and only if all possible connectives can be expressed in terms of the given ones. Truth functional completeness is an extremely important property; a logical system that didn't satisfy it would be like a system of arithmetic that had no support for certain operations, say the operation of addition.

truth functional equivalence Logical equivalence, q.v.

truth functional implication Logical implication, q.v.

truth table Let X be a propositional expression. Then the semantics of X can be defined by means of a truth table that shows, for each possible combination of truth values for the propositional variables in X, the truth value of the overall expression.

Example: Let X be the expression $(p$ AND $q)$ OR r, where p, q, and r are propositional variables. Then, using T and F to represent TRUE and FALSE, respectively, the semantics of X are as defined by the following self-explanatory truth table:

p	q	r	p AND q	(p AND q) OR r
T	T	T	T	T
T	T	F	T	T
T	F	T	F	T
T	F	F	F	F
F	T	T	F	T
F	T	F	F	F
F	F	T	F	T
F	F	F	F	F

truth value In two-valued logic, either TRUE or FALSE; in other words, a Boolean value. *Note*: Many-valued logics, q.v., support additional "truth values" over and above the conventional TRUE and FALSE.

truth value of In logic, an operator (in symbols, "/. . ./") that, given a logical expression, returns the truth value of that expression. For example, let the symbols x and y denote integers. Then the expression $/x > y/$ returns TRUE if the integer denoted by x is greater than that denoted by y and FALSE otherwise. Note that /TRUE/ and /FALSE/ return TRUE and FALSE, respectively. Note too that the logical expression p EQUIV q means the same as $/p/ = /q/$; for example, the expression (Neptune is a planet) EQUIV (Mars has exactly two moons) means the same as the expression /(Neptune is a planet)/ = /(Mars has exactly two moons)/. Note further that (at least in the computing literature) authors often write $p = q$ when what they really mean is $/p/ = /q/$; *caveat lector*.

truth valued expression A logical expression, q.v.

truth valued operator A read-only logical operator, q.v. (especially one of the connectives, q.v.).

tuple A tuple value, q.v.

tuple (mathematics) Given sets *s1, s2,* . . ., *sn,* not necessarily distinct, *t* is an *n*-tuple (tuple for short) on those sets if and only if it's an ordered collection of elements, the first of which is from *s1,* the second from *s2,* and so on. Set *si* is the *i*th domain of *t* ($i = 1, \ldots, n$). *Note:* There are several important logical differences between tuples in mathematics and their relational model counterparts. *See* relation (mathematics); tuple value.

tuple assignment An operation that assigns a tuple value to a tuple variable (of the same type). *See* assignment.

tuple calculus A form of relational calculus, semantically equivalent to domain calculus, q.v., in which the range variables range over relations and thus denote tuples from those relations.

Example: Here's a tuple calculus formulation of the query "Get supplier names for suppliers who supply at least one part" (*see* domain calculus for a domain calculus analog):

```
SX   RANGES OVER { S } ;
SPX  RANGES OVER { SP } ;


SX.SNAME WHERE EXISTS SPX ( SPX.S# = SX.S# )
```

In stilted English: "Get names of suppliers SX where there exists a shipment SPX with the same supplier number as SX."

tuple comparison A Boolean expression of the form (*exp1*) *theta* (*exp2*), where *exp1* and *exp2* are tuple expressions of the same type and *theta* is either "=" or "≠" (observe that the operators "<" and ">" are explicitly not defined for tuples). *Note:* The parentheses enclosing *exp1* and *exp2* in the comparison might not be needed in practice.

tuple component An <attribute, attribute value> pair appearing in the tuple in question. Note that attributes in turn are defined to be <attribute name, type name> pairs. However, other formalisms are possible; for example, it would be possible to define a tuple component as an <attribute name, type name, attribute value> triple instead of an <attribute, attribute value> pair. (As a matter of fact, *The Third Manifesto* does exactly this.) Of course, it's easy to see that these two formalisms are isomorphic.

Examples: The pairs <<S#,S#>,S1> and <<SNAME,NAME>,Smith> are both components of the supplier tuple for supplier S1 in Figure 1. *Note*: In **Tutorial D**, tuple components are specified more simply as <attribute name, attribute value> pairs (not meant to be exact **Tutorial D** syntax). This simplified form is acceptable because the relational model requires attribute names to be unique within the pertinent heading, and those names thus effectively imply the corresponding type names.

tuple composition The tuple composition of tuples *t1* and *t2*, *t1* COMPOSE *t2*, is the tuple union of *t1* and *t2*, projected on all attributes not common to *t1* and *t2*.

tuple constant A tuple, especially one that's named; not to be confused with a tuple literal, q.v.

tuple constraint Slightly deprecated term sometimes used to refer to a relvar constraint of the form IS_EMPTY(*R* WHERE *bx*), where *R* is a relvar and *bx* is a restriction condition, q.v., on *R* (and can therefore be evaluated for a given tuple by examining just that tuple in isolation). Note that a tuple constraint is indeed a constraint on a relvar and not on a tuplevar. (There aren't any tuplevars in a relational database; a fortiori, therefore, there aren't any "tuplevar constraints" either.)

Example: Constraints C1 and C2 from the examples under database constraint are both tuple constraints; constraint C3 is not.

tuple difference *See* tuple union.

tuple equality Equality of tuples; tuples *t1* and *t2* are equal (i.e., the tuple comparison *t1* = *t2* evaluates to TRUE) if and only if *t1* and *t2* are the very same tuple. More specifically, tuples *t1* and *t2* are equal if and only if they have the same attributes *A1, A2, . . ., An*—in other words, they're of the same type—and, for all i ($i = 1, 2, \ldots, n$), the value $v1$ of Ai in $t1$ is equal to the value $v2$ of Ai in $t2$. *Note*: The importance of this concept can hardly be overstated, since so much in the relational model depends on it. For example, candidate keys, foreign keys, and most if not all of the operators of relational algebra are defined in terms of it. Note in particular too that (speaking somewhat loosely) all 0-tuples are equal to one another, since in fact there's only one such tuple.

tuple expression An expression denoting a tuple. Tuple literals, tuple selector invocations, tuplevar references, and read-only tuple operator invocations are all special cases.

tuple extension Let t be a tuple. Then the tuple extension EXTEND t ADD (*exp* AS X) is a tuple identical to t except that it has an additional attribute called X, with value as specified by *exp*. Tuple t must not have an attribute called X, and *exp* must not refer to X.

Example: Let t be some tuple from relvar P. Then the expression

```
EXTEND t ADD ( WEIGHT * 454 AS GMWT )
```

yields a tuple just like t, except that it has an additional attribute GMWT ("gram weight") whose value is 454 times the WEIGHT value in that same tuple.

tuple extractor An operator for extracting the single tuple from a specified relation of cardinality one.

Example: The following expression extracts the supplier tuple for supplier S1 from the current value of relvar S:

```
TUPLE FROM ( S WHERE S# = S#('S1') )
```

A run-time error will occur if the TUPLE FROM argument doesn't have cardinality exactly one.

TUPLE FROM **Tutorial D** syntax for a tuple extractor, q.v.

tuple ID *See* row ID.

tuple intersection *See* tuple union.

tuple join *See* tuple union.

tuple level An operator is tuple level if it takes individual tuples or tuplevars or both as operands and either produces a tuple as a result or updates a tuple variable. There are no tuple level operators in the relational model as such, but such operators are likely to be needed in the external environment in order to support, e.g., extraction of some tuple from some relation. (By contrast, SQL in particular supports certain tuple level operations—specifically, DELETE WHERE CURRENT and UPDATE WHERE CURRENT—that aren't just part of the external environment but are supposed to affect the database directly. The operators in question thus constitute a departure from the relational model.)

tuple literal A literal that denotes a tuple.

Examples: See the examples under literal.

tuple operator An operator that (a) takes either tuples or tuplevars (or both) as operands and (b) either returns a tuple or updates at least one tuplevar.

tuple projection Let t be a tuple and let $\{X\}$ be a subset of the heading of t. Then the tuple projection of t on $\{X\}$, $t\{X\}$, is a tuple obtained from t by removing all components not corresponding to attributes in $\{X\}$.

Example: Let t be some tuple in relvar S. Then the expression $t\{STATUS,CITY\}$ yields a tuple of type TUPLE {STATUS INTEGER, CITY CHAR}, containing just the STATUS and CITY components from that tuple t.

tuple relational calculus Tuple calculus, q.v.

tuple renaming Let t be a tuple, let A be an attribute of t, and let t not have an attribute named B. Then the tuple renaming t RENAME (A AS B) is a tuple identical to t except that attribute A in that tuple is renamed B.

Example: Let *t* be some tuple from relvar P. Then the expression

```
t RENAME ( WEIGHT AS WT )
```

yields a tuple just like *t,* except that attribute WEIGHT is renamed WT.

tuple selector *See* selector.

tuple type Let {*H*} be a heading; then TUPLE {*H*} is a tuple type with the same degree and attributes as {*H*}.

Examples: The type of the tuples in relvar S is

```
TUPLE { S# S#,  SNAME NAME,
                STATUS INTEGER, CITY CHAR }
```

The following (corresponding to a certain projection of a supplier tuple) is also a tuple type:

```
TUPLE { CITY CHAR, SNAME NAME }
```

tuple type generator *See* type generator.

tuple type inference The process of determining the type of the value denoted by a given tuple expression. Note that this process is completely specified by the rules defining the types of the results of the various tuple operations, q.v.

tuple union Let tuples *t1* and *t2* be such that attributes with the same name are of the same type and have the same value. Then the tuple union of *t1* and *t2, t1* UNION *t2,* is the set theory union of *t1* and *t2.* (This operation could obviously be generalized to apply to any number of tuples.)
Note: Tuple union might reasonably be called tuple join. Also, it would clearly be possible to define tuple intersection and tuple difference operators if desired.

Example: Let *t1* be a tuple from relvar S and *t2* a tuple from relvar SP, and let *t1* and *t2* have the same S# component (the same S# value in particular). Then the expression *t1* UNION *t2* yields a tuple of type TUPLE {S# S#,

SNAME NAME, STATUS INTEGER, CITY CHAR, P# P#, QTY QTY},
with components as in *t1* or *t2* or both, as applicable.

tuple unwrapping Let *s* be a tuple with an attribute *YT* of type TUPLE
{*Y*}, and let {*X*} be the set of all attributes of *s* except *YT*. Let {*Y*} have
attributes *Y1, Y2, . . ., Yn*; also, let {*X*} not contain any attribute with the
same name as any of *Y1, Y2, . . ., Yn*. Then the tuple unwrapping *s*
UNWRAP (*YT*) is another tuple *t*. The heading of *t* consists of the set
theory union of {*X*} and {*Y*}. Let tuple *s* have *X* value *x* and *YT* value a
tuple with *Y1* value *y1, Y2* value *y2, . . .,* and *Yn* value *yn*; then tuple *t* has *X*
value *x, Y1* value *y1, Y2* value *y2, . . .,* and *Yn* value *yn*.

Example: Let *t* be a tuple from relvar SP, and let *tw* be the tuple resulting
from the expression

```
t WRAP ( { P#, QTY } AS PQ_TUP )
```

(*see* tuple wrapping). Then the expression

```
tw UNWRAP ( PQ_TUP )
```

yields *t*.

tuple value Loosely, a row (value). More precisely, let TUPLE {*H*} be a
tuple type, and let *t* be a set of pairs <<*A,T*>,*v*>, called components (q.v.),
obtained from {*H*} by attaching to each attribute <*A,T*> in {*H*} some value
v of type *T*, called the attribute value in *t* for attribute *A*. Then *t* is a tuple
value (tuple for short) of type TUPLE {*H*}, with heading {*H*} and the same
degree and attributes as {*H*}. *Note*: Tuples as defined in the relational
model differ in certain important respects from the mathematical construct
of the same name. In particular, tuples in mathematics typically don't have
named attributes; instead, their attributes are identified by their ordinal
position, left to right. *See* tuple (mathematics).

tuple valued attribute An attribute whose type is some tuple type.
Values of such an attribute are tuples of the specified type. *Note*: If a
relvar has a tuple valued attribute, that fact in and of itself doesn't

constitute a violation of any particular level of normalization (not even first); however, such attributes are usually contraindicated in database design, at least in base relvars, because they necessarily imply some structural asymmetry and thereby give rise to asymmetry (and complexity) in queries, constraints, and updates as well. *See also* tuple unwrapping; tuple wrapping.

tuple variable Loosely, a row (variable); more precisely, a variable whose type is some tuple type. Let tuple variable T be of type TUPLE $\{H\}$; then T has the same heading (and therefore attributes) and degree as that type does. *Note*: Tuple variables aren't required by the relational model as such, but they're likely to be needed in the external environment in order to support, for example, extraction of some tuple from some relation.

tuple wrapping Let t be a tuple and let the heading of t be partitioned into subsets $\{X\}$ and $\{Y\}$. Let the attributes of $\{Y\}$ be $Y1, Y2, \ldots, Yn$; also, let $\{X\}$ not contain any attribute called YT. Then the tuple wrapping t WRAP ($\{Y\}$ AS YT) is another tuple s. The heading of s consists of $\{X\}$ extended with an attribute YT of type TUPLE $\{Y\}$. Let tuple t have X value x, $Y1$ value $y1$, $Y2$ value $y2$, $\ldots$, and Yn value yn; then tuple s has X value x and YT value a tuple with $Y1$ value $y1$, $Y2$ value $y2$, $\ldots$, and Yn value yn.

Example: Let t be the tuple for supplier S1 and part P1 from relvar SP. Then the expression

```
t WRAP ( { P#, QTY } AS PQ_TUP )
```

yields a tuple *tw* of type TUPLE $\{$S# S#, PQ_TUP TUPLE $\{$P# P#, QTY QTY$\}\}$, with S# value S1 and PQ_TUP value a tuple with P# value P1 and QTY value 300.

tuplevar A tuple variable, q.v.

tuplevar reference Syntactically, a tuplevar name, used to denote either the tuplevar as such or the value of that tuplevar, as the context demands.

Tutorial D A particular **D**, q.v. (see the introduction to this dictionary).

TVA Tuple valued attribute.

two-valued logic Conventional propositional or predicate logic, in which there are just two truth values, TRUE and FALSE; abbreviated 2VL.

type A named set of values; not to be confused with the internal or physical representation of the values in question, which is an implementation issue. Every value, every variable, every attribute, every read-only operator, every parameter, and every expression is of some type. Types can be either scalar or nonscalar (in particular, they can be tuple or relation types); as a consequence, attributes of relations can also be either scalar or nonscalar. Types can also be either system defined (i.e., built in) or user defined. They can also be generated (*see* type generator).
Note: A type isn't a value, nor is it a variable; in particular, relation values and relation variables aren't types. Equating types and either relation values or relation variables—positions that have been advocated in the literature—has been described as The First Great Blunder. (For the second, *see* pointer; Second Great Blunder, The.)

Example: Here's a sample type definition:

```
TYPE POINT ...
    { ... CONSTRAINT ( X↑2 + Y↑2 ) ≤ 10000 } ;
```

POINT here is a user defined type, denoting geometric points in two-dimensional space. It's subject to a type constraint that says, in effect, that the only points of interest are those that lie on or inside a circle with center the origin and radius 100 (the symbol "↑" denotes exponentiation).
Note: The (necessary) definition of the representation of POINT values in terms of the Cartesian coordinates X and Y is deliberately omitted from the example, since a detailed discussion of that definition would take us too far afield. Other irrelevant details are also omitted for similar reasons.

type constraint A definition of the set of values that make up a given type. The type constraint for type T is checked when some selector is invoked for that type T; in other words, a type constraint error occurs if and only if some selector is invoked with arguments that violate the applicable type constraint. *Contrast* type error.

Example: *See* the example under type.

type error The error that occurs if some operator is invoked with an argument not of the type of the corresponding parameter. Unlike integrity violations, such errors should be detectable at compile time (unless type inheritance is supported, in which case certain type errors—not all, by any means—might not be detectable until run time).

type generator An operator that's invoked at compile time instead of run time and returns a type instead of a value. For example, conventional programming languages typically support an array type generator, which lets users define a variety of specific array types. In the relational model, the tuple and (especially) relation type generators are the most important ones; they allow users to define a variety of specific tuple and relation types. *See* relation type; tuple type.

Example: Consider the suppliers relvar definition:

```
VAR S BASE RELATION
   { S# S#, SNAME NAME, STATUS INTEGER, CITY CHAR }
     KEY { S# } ;
```

This definition includes an invocation of the RELATION type generator (syntactically, everything from the keyword RELATION to the closing brace following the keyword CHAR, inclusive). That invocation returns a specific relation type—namely, the type

```
RELATION
   { S# S#, SNAME NAME, STATUS INTEGER, CITY CHAR }
```

So this type is in fact a generated type—as indeed are all relation types, and all tuple types also.

type inference The process of determining the type of the value denoted by a given expression. Note that this process is completely specified by the rules defining the types of the results of the various operations involved in the expression in question (in fact, of course, the type of the value denoted by expression x is, precisely, the type of the result of the outermost operation involved in x).

type inheritance An organizing principle according to which one type can be defined as a subtype of one or more other types, called supertypes (of the type in question). If $T2$ is a (proper) subtype of supertype $T1$, then all values of type $T2$ are also of type $T1$, and read-only operators and type constraints that apply to values of type $T1$ are inherited by values of type $T2$. However, values of type $T2$ will have read-only operators and type constraints of their own that don't apply to values that are only of type $T1$ and not $T2$.

U

UDO User defined operator.

UDT User defined type.

unary Of degree one.

UNGROUP *See* ungrouping.

ungrouping Let *s* be a relation with an attribute *YR* of type RELATION {*Y*}, and let {*X*} be the set of all attributes of *s* except *YR*. Let {*Y*} have attributes *Y1, Y2, . . ., Yn*; also, let {*X*} not contain any attribute with the same name as any of *Y1, Y2, . . ., Yn*. Then the ungrouping *s* UNGROUP (*YR*) is another relation *r*. The heading of *r* consists of the set theory union of {*X*} and {*Y*}. As for the body, let *z* be a relation with heading consisting of {*X*} extended with an attribute *YT*, of type TUPLE {*Y*}, and body defined as follows: for each tuple of *s*, *z* contains a set of tuples, one (*t*, say) for each tuple in the *YR* value in that *s* tuple; each such tuple *t* contains an *X* value (*x*, say) equal to the *X* value from the *s* tuple in question and a tuple value (*yt*, say) equal to some tuple from the *YR* value in the *s* tuple in question. Let *z* contain no other tuples. Then *r* is the result of *z* UNWRAP (*YT*).

Example: Let *spq* be the relation resulting from the expression

    SP GROUP ({ P#, QTY } AS PQ_REL)

(*see* grouping). Then the expression

    spq UNGROUP (PQ_REL)

denotes an ungrouping of *spq*. That ungrouping is a relation of type RELATION {S# S#, P# P#, QTY QTY}; and if *spq* is obtained from the relation *sp* shown as the value of relvar SP in Figure 1, then the result of ungrouping *spq* is just *sp*. Suppose, however, that *spq* additionally contains a tuple, say for supplier S5, in which the PQ_REL value is an empty relation; then the result of the foregoing UNGROUP won't contain a tuple for supplier S5 (in fact, the result will still be, exactly, relation *sp*). In general, therefore, ungrouping a relation *r* and then grouping it again in what might look like an inverse way isn't guaranteed to take us back to *r* (*contrast* grouping).

uniform representation *See* Information Principle, The.

UNION *See* union.

union 1. (*Dyadic case*) The union of two relations *r1* and *r2*, *r1* UNION *r2*, where *r1* and *r2* are of the same type *T*, is a relation of type *T* with body the set of all tuples *t* such that *t* appears in either or both of *r1* and *r2*. 2. (*N-adic case*) The union of *n* relations *r1, r2, . . ., rn* ($n \geq 0$), UNION {*r1,r2,. . .,rn*}, where *r1, r2, . . ., rn* are all of the same type *T*, is a relation of type *T* with body the set of all tuples *t* such that *t* appears in at least one of *r1, r2, . . ., rn*. *Note*: If $n = 0$, (a) some syntactic mechanism, not shown here, is needed to specify the pertinent type *T* and (b) the result is the empty relation of that type. Note too that the relational union operator differs in certain respects from the mathematical or set theory operator of the same name, q.v. *See also* disjoint union; tuple union.

Example: The expression (S{CITY}) UNION (P{CITY}) denotes the union of the projections on {CITY} of the relations that are the current values of relvars S and P. That union is a relation of type RELATION {CITY CHAR}. Moreover, if the current values of relvars S and P are *s* and *p*, respectively, the body of that relation consists of all tuples of the form <*c*> that appear in *s*{CITY} or *p*{CITY} or both—meaning *c* is a current supplier city or a current part city or both.

union (bag theory) *See* bag.

union (set theory) The set of all elements appearing in either or both of two given sets. *Note*: This definition can obviously be extended to apply to any number of sets.

union compatibility (*Of relations*) Of the same type. The term is deprecated for many reasons, of which inappropriateness is one.

union plus *See* bag.

UNIQUE Keyword sometimes used to denote the quantifier "there exists exactly one of."

Example: Here's a tuple calculus formulation of the foreign key constraint "Every shipment has exactly one corresponding supplier":

```
SX   RANGES OVER { S }  ;
SPX RANGES OVER { SP }  ;


CONSTRAINT SP_REFERENCES_S
    FORALL SPX ( UNIQUE SX ( SX.S# = SPX.S# ) ) ;
```

unique index An index—hence, an implementation construct—on (the stored analog of) some relvar on the basis of some key for that relvar; not to be confused with the key as such, even though the index might be used to implement the corresponding key constraint.

universal quantifier Let $p(x)$ be a predicate with a parameter x; then FORALL x ($p(x)$ is a predicate, and it means "for all arguments v that can replace the parameter x, $p(v)$ is true." In this example, FORALL x is a universal quantifier, and x is a universally quantified bound variable, q.v. *Note*: Some writers refer to FORALL by itself as the quantifier; the literature is not consistent on this point. More important, note that if $v1$, $v2$, . . ., vn are all of the possible arguments in the foregoing example, then FORALL x ($p(x)$) is equivalent to ($p(v1)$) AND ($p(v2)$) AND . . . AND ($p(vn)$) AND TRUE. Observe in particular that this expression evaluates to TRUE if $n = 0$ (i.e., if the bound variable x ranges over an empty set). Observe further that the expression FORALL x ($p(x)$) is logically equivalent to the expression NOT (EXISTS x (NOT ($p(x)$))). *Contrast* existential quantifier.

Example: Here's a tuple calculus query that makes use of the universal quantifier as well as the existential quantifier ("Get suppliers who supply all parts"):

```
SX   RANGES OVER { S }  ;
SPX  RANGES OVER { SP } ;
PX   RANGES OVER { P }  ;

SX WHERE
    FORALL PX ( EXISTS SPX ( SPX.S# = SX.S# AND
                             SPX.P# = PX.P# ) )
```

This latter expression can be read as "Suppliers SX where for all parts PX there exists a shipment SPX with the same supplier number as SX and the same part number as PX."

universal relation Given a relation type RELATION {*H*}, the relation of that type that contains all possible tuples of type TUPLE {*H*}. Note, therefore, that there's exactly one universal relation for each relation type. *Contrast* empty relation.

universal relvar The join of all relvars in a given set of relvars. The normalization procedure of nonloss decomposition, if viewed in isolation (i.e., ignoring other possible aids to database design), tacitly assumes that it's possible to define an initial universal relvar that has all of the attributes relevant to the database under consideration, and then shows how that relvar can be replaced by successively "smaller" (i.e., lower degree) projections until a "good" design is reached.

universal set The set that contains all of the elements of interest in some given context.

universe of discourse *See* sorted logic.

unnormalized Not normalized (i.e., not in first normal form, q.v.); not to be confused with denormalized (*see* denormalization).

unsorted logic *See* sorted logic.

UNWRAP *See* unwrapping.

unwrapping Let *s* be a relation with an attribute *YT* of type TUPLE {*Y*}, and {*X*} be the set of all attributes of *s* except *YT*. Let {*Y*} have attributes *Y1, Y2, . . ., Yn*; also, let {*X*} not contain any attribute with the same name as any of *Y1, Y2, . . ., Yn*. Then the unwrapping *s* UNWRAP (*YT*) is another relation *r*. The heading of *r* consists of the set theory union of {*X*} and {*Y*}. The body of *r* contains one tuple for each tuple in *s*, and no other tuples. Let tuple *t* of *s* have *X* value *x* and *YT* value a tuple with *Y1* value *y1, Y2* value *y2, . . .,* and *Yn* value *yn*; then the corresponding tuple of *r* has *X* value *x, Y1* value *y1, Y2* value *y2, . . .,* and *Yn* value *yn*. *See also* tuple unwrapping.

Example: Let *spw* be the relation resulting from the expression

```
SP WRAP ( { P#, QTY } AS PQ_REL )
```

(*see* wrapping). Then the following expression denotes an unwrapping of *spw*:

```
spw UNWRAP ( PQ_REL )
```

That unwrapping is a relation of type RELATION {S# S#, P# P#, QTY QTY}. If *spw* is obtained by wrapping the relation *sp* shown as the value of relvar SP in Figure 1, then the result of unwrapping *spw* is just *sp*.

UPDATE 1. (*Read-only operator*) *See* what if. 2. (*Update operator*) Very loosely, an operator that updates a given set of attributes in a given set of tuples in a given relvar; slightly less loosely, an operator that replaces a given set of tuples in a given relvar with another such set. It's shorthand for a certain relational assignment.

Example (second definition only): The UPDATE statement

```
UPDATE P WHERE CITY = 'London' :
      { WEIGHT := 2 * WEIGHT , CITY := 'Oslo' } ;
```

is shorthand for the following relational assignment:

```
P := WITH ( P WHERE CITY = 'London' ) AS t1 ,
          ( EXTEND t1 ADD
               ( 2 * WEIGHT AS NW ) ) AS t2 ,
          ( EXTEND t2 ADD
               ( 'Oslo' AS NC ) ) AS t3 ,
          ( t3 { P#, PNAME, COLOR, NW, NC } ) AS t4 ,
          ( t4 RENAME ( NW AS WEIGHT ) ) AS t5 ,
          ( t5 RENAME ( NC AS CITY ) ) AS t6 ,
          ( P MINUS t1 ) AS t7 :
     t7 UNION t6 ;
```

In this example, we might say, loosely, that attributes WEIGHT and CITY are being updated in the tuples for London parts; we might also say, still loosely but a little less so, that the tuples for London parts are being replaced; but what's really happening is that a certain relation value is being assigned to a certain relation variable.

UPDATE rule A foreign key rule, q.v., that specifies the action to be taken by the DBMS if some tuple *t2* exists that contains a foreign key value referencing some tuple *t1* and—speaking very loosely (*see* tuple level)—the corresponding candidate key in tuple *t1* is updated.

update A relational assignment (especially an INSERT, DELETE, or UPDATE operation).

update anomaly A somewhat old fashioned term, never very precisely defined, for the kind of thing that can go wrong in a less than fully normalized database (or, more generally, in any database that involves uncontrolled redundancy).

update operator An operator that, when invoked, returns no value but updates at least one variable (usually an argument) that's not local to the implementation of the operator in question. An update operator invocation has no value—thus, it's not an expression, and it can't appear wherever an expression is required. In particular, it can't be nested inside expressions.

Every update operator invocation is semantically equivalent to some assignment (possibly a multiple assignment, q.v.).

Example: See the second example under argument.

update propagation *See* controlled redundancy.

user Either an end user or an application programmer or both, as the context demands.

user defined Defined by some agency other than the system; i.e., not system defined (not built in). User defined operators and user defined types provide obvious examples. *Note*: The term "user defined" is sanctioned by usage but really isn't very good. Consider the case of a user defined type T, for example. To the user who merely makes use of that type—as opposed to the user who actually defines it—type T behaves in all major respects just like a system defined type (indeed, that's the whole point). In other words, what's being sought is not so much a distinction between the user and the system as it is a distinction between different roles played by users (possibly by the same user) in different contexts.

V

value An "individual constant" (e.g., the integer value 3). Values can be of arbitrary complexity (they can be scalar or nonscalar; note in particular that tuples and relations are both values). Values have no location in time or space; however, they can be represented in memory by means of some encoding, and those representations do have locations in time and space—indeed, distinct representations of the same value can appear at any number of distinct locations in time and space, meaning, loosely, that the same value can appear as the current value of any number of distinct variables, and/or as any number of attribute values within the current value of any number of distinct tuplevars or relvars, at the same time or different times. Note that, by definition, a value can't be updated; for if it could, then after such an update it would no longer be that value. Note too that every value is of some type (in fact, of exactly one type, except possibly if type inheritance is supported). Note further that a value isn't a type, nor is it a variable. *Contrast* appearance.

value set Term sometimes used in E/R modeling to mean a type.

VAR The **Tutorial D** operator for defining variables (relation variables in particular).

variable 1. (*Logic*) *See* logic variable. 2. (*Programming languages*) A holder for a representation of a value, q.v. Unlike values, variables (a) do have location in time and space and (b) can be updated (that is, the current value of the variable can be replaced by another value). Indeed, to be a variable is to be updatable; equivalently, to be a variable is to be assignable to (and to be assignable to is to be a variable). Note that every variable is declared to be of some type. Note further that a variable isn't a type, nor is it a value.

variable reference 1. (*Logic*) *See* bound variable; free variable.
2. (*Programming languages*) Syntactically, a variable name (except as
noted under pseudovariable reference), used to denote either the variable as
such or the value of that variable, as the context demands. Note that such a
reference certainly denotes the variable as such if it's used to specify a
target for some update operation—in particular, if it appears on the left side
of an assignment. If on the other hand it denotes the value of the variable,
then it can be regarded as an invocation of a read-only operator—and hence
as a special case of an expression, q.v.—where the read-only operator in
question is essentially "return the current value of the specified variable."
Note: If the variable reference *V* in fact denotes the value of *V*, then (like
all expressions) it can appear wherever a literal of the appropriate type can
appear. *See also* pseudovariable reference.

vertical decomposition Informal term for decomposition into projections.

view A derived relvar that's virtual, not real (*contrast* snapshot).
The value of a given view at a given time is the result of evaluating a
certain relational expression (the view defining expression, specified when
the view per se is defined) at the time in question. *Note*: The view
defining expression must mention at least one relvar, for otherwise the
view wouldn't be, specifically, a relation variable. Note too that the view
must be updatable for the same reason.

Example: The following statement defines a view called LSV:

```
VAR LSV VIRTUAL ( S WHERE CITY = 'London' ) ;
```

The relation that's the value of view LSV at any given time is equal to the
value of the view defining expression S WHERE CITY = 'London' at that
time.

view materialization A somewhat unsophisticated technique for implementing operations on views according to which (a) the relational expression that defines the view is evaluated at the time the operation is invoked, (b) a relation is thereby materialized, and (c) the operation in question is then executed against the relation so materialized. Observe that this technique can't be used for implementing view updates but is limited to read-only operations. *Contrast* substitution (second definition). *See also* materialized view.

view updating Either the theory or the process of updating views, as the context demands. View updating is still a somewhat controversial topic, but there are those who believe that—contrary to popular opinion—all views are at least theoretically updatable. The details are beyond the scope of this dictionary, except to note that (a) a view update can fail on an integrity violation, of course, just as a base relvar update can, and (b) an argument can be made that view updates that are regarded by some as "impossible" aren't intrinsically impossible but instead fail on just such a violation.

virtual relation The value of a given virtual relvar at a given time.

virtual relvar A view, q.v. (*contrast* real relvar).

W

well-formed formula In logic, a formal expression denoting a predicate.

WFF A well-formed formula. The abbreviation is variously pronounced "weff" or "wiff" or "woof." *See* closed WFF; open WFF.

what if A read-only relational operator that returns the relation that would result if certain changes were made to a specified relation (ignoring the fact that such changes couldn't in fact be made, because a relation is a value).

Example: Consider the following expression:

```
UPDATE S WHERE CITY = 'Paris' :
    { STATUS := 2 * STATUS , CITY := 'Nice' }
```

Observe that, even though it uses the keyword UPDATE, this expression is indeed an expression and not a statement (it has no terminating semicolon); in particular, it has no effect on relvar S. What it does do is return a relation containing exactly one tuple *t* for each tuple *s* in the current value of relvar S for which the city is Paris—except that, in that tuple *t,* the status is double that in tuple *s* and the city is Nice, not Paris.

WHERE clause A syntactic construct of the form WHERE *bx* (where *bx* is a Boolean expression) that appears ubiquitously in **Tutorial D**, SQL, and many other languages. *See* DELETE; restriction; restriction condition; SELECT expression; UPDATE; and elsewhere.

WITH A **Tutorial D** syntactic construct for introducing names for the results of subexpressions. The introduced names are then available for subsequent use within the overall expression of which the WITH clause forms a part to denote those results. (SQL also includes a WITH construct, with similar but not identical semantics.)

Example: The following is a formulation of the query "Get pairs of supplier numbers, S*x* and S*y* say, such that S*x* and S*y* each supply exactly the same set of parts":

```
WITH ( S RENAME ( S# AS SX ) ) { SX } AS tx ,
     ( S RENAME ( S# AS SY ) ) { SY } AS ty :
( tx JOIN ty ) WHERE ( SP WHERE S# = SX ) { P# } =
                     ( SP WHERE S# = SY ) { P# }
```

WRAP *See* wrapping.

wrapping Let *r* be a relation and let the heading of *r* be partitioned into subsets {*X*} and {*Y*}. Let the attributes of {*Y*} be *Y1, Y2, . . ., Yn*; also, let {*X*} not contain any attribute called *YT*. Then the wrapping *r* WRAP ({*Y*} AS *YT*) is another relation *s*. The heading of *s* consists of {*X*} extended with an attribute *YT* of type TUPLE {*Y*}. The body of *s* contains one tuple for each tuple in *r,* and no other tuples. Let tuple *t* of *r* have *X* value *x, Y1* value *y1, Y2* value *y2, . . .,* and *Yn* value *yn*; then the corresponding tuple of *s* has *X* value *x* and *YT* value a tuple with *Y1* value *y1, Y2* value *y2, . . .,* and *Yn* value *yn. See also* tuple wrapping.

Example: The following expression denotes a wrapping of the relation that's the current value of relvar SP:

```
SP WRAP ( { P#, QTY } AS PQ_TUP )
```

That wrapping is a relation *spw* of type RELATION {S# S#, PQ_TUP TUPLE {P# P#, QTY QTY}}; it contains one tuple for each tuple currently appearing in relvar SP, and no other tuples. Given the sample values in Figure 1, for example, the *spw* tuple for supplier S1 and part P1 has S# value S1 and PQ_TUP value a tuple with P# value P1 and QTY value 300.

X

XML Extensible Markup Language; from a database point of view, best regarded as just another data type (albeit one of considerable pragmatic importance at the time of writing)—meaning, among other things, that relations should be allowed to have attributes of the type in question, and tuples in such relations should thus be allowed to contain attribute values that are XML documents.

XOR *See* exclusive OR.

Copyright

The Relational Database Dictionary, Extended Edition

© 2008 by C. J. Date

ISBN-13 (electronic): 978-1-4302-1042-9

ISBN-13 (paperback): 978-1-4302-1041-2

Distributed to the book trade in the United States by Springer-Verlag New York, Inc., 233 Spring Street, 6th Floor, New York, NY 10013, and outside the United States by Springer-Verlag GmbH & Co. KG, Tiergartenstr. 17, 69112 Heidelberg, Germany.

In the United States: phone 1-800-SPRINGER, fax 201-348-4505, e-mail orders@springer-ny.com, or visit http://www.springer-ny.com. Outside the United States: fax +49 6221 345229, e-mail orders@springer.de, or visit http://www.springer.de.

For information on translations, please contact Apress directly at 2855 Telegraph Ave, Suite 600, Berkeley, CA 94705. Phone 510-549-5930, fax 510-549-5939, e-mail info@apress.com, or visit http://www.apress.com.

Printed in the United States
120509LV00003B/1-66/P